Learning and Research in Virtual Worlds

Virtual worlds are places where humans interact, and as such they can be environments for research and learning. These environments are complex and mutable in ways that more controlled and traditional environments are not. Although computer-mediated, virtual worlds are multifaceted social systems like the offline world, choosing to study virtual world phenomena demands as much consideration for the participants, the environment and the researcher as any environment.

By exploring virtual worlds as places of research and learning, the international practitioners in this book demonstrate the power of these worlds to replicate and extend our arenas of research and learning. They focus on process and outcomes considering questions that arise from engaging in teaching and research in these spaces, including new approaches to research ethics, internationalization, localization, and collaboration in virtual worlds.

This book was originally published as a special issue of *Learning, Media & Technology*.

Jeremy Hunsinger is Assistant Professor of Communication Studies at Wilfrid Laurier University, Canada.

Aleks Krotoski is a Visiting Fellow in the Media & Communications Department at the London School of Economics. She is also a Research Associate at the Oxford Internet Institute, and writes for The Guardian and Observer newspapers. She is based in London, UK.

Learning and Research in Virtual Worlds

Edited by
Jeremy Hunsinger and Aleks Krotoski

LONDON AND NEW YORK

First published 2012
by Routledge
2 Park Square, Milton Park, Abingdon, Oxfordshire OX14 4RN

Simultaneously published in the USA and Canada
by Routledge
711 Third Avenue, New York, NY 10017

First issued in paperback 2014

Routledge is an imprint of the Taylor and Francis Group, an informa company

© 2012 Taylor & Francis

This book is a reproduction of *Learning, Media & Technology*, volume 35, issue 2. The Publisher requests to those authors who may be citing this book to state, also, the bibliographical details of the special issue on which the book was based.

All rights reserved. No part of this book may be reprinted or reproduced or utilised in any form or by any electronic, mechanical, or other means, now known or hereafter invented, including photocopying and recording, or in any information storage or retrieval system, without permission in writing from the publishers.

Trademark notice: Product or corporate names may be trademarks or registered trademarks, and are used only for identification and explanation without intent to infringe.

British Library Cataloguing in Publication Data
A catalogue record for this book is available from the British Library

ISBN13: 978-0-415-69347-9 (hbk)
ISBN13: 978-0-415-75460-6 (pbk)

Typeset in Times New Roman
by Taylor & Francis Books

Publisher's Note
The publisher would like to make readers aware that the chapters in this book may be referred to as articles as they are identical to the articles published in the special issue. The publisher accepts responsibility for any inconsistencies that may have arisen in the course of preparing this volume for print.

Contents

Notes on contributors vii

1. Learning and researching in virtual worlds
   Jeremy Hunsinger and Aleks Krotoski 1

2. *Immersed in Learning*: supporting creative practice in virtual worlds
   Denise Doyle 7

3. Design of learning spaces in 3D virtual worlds: an empirical investigation of *Second Life*
   Shailey Minocha and Ahmad John Reeves 19

4. Social virtual worlds for technology-enhanced learning on an augmented learning platform
   Li Jin, Zhigang Wen and Norman Gough 46

5. How to enable knowledge exchange in *Second Life* in design education?
   Aukje Thomassen and Pete Rive 61

6. 'Elven Elder LVL59 LFP/RB. Please PM me': immersion, collaborative tasks and problem-solving in massively multiplayer online games
   Iro Voulgari and Vassilis Komis 76

7. Serious playground: using *Second Life* to engage high school students in urban planning
   Kerry Mallan, Marcus Foth, Ruth Greenaway and Greg T. Young 107

8. The city at play: *Second Life* and the virtual urban planning studio
   David Thomas and Justin B. Hollander 130

9. The potential for scientific collaboration in virtual ecosystems
   Brian Magerko 146

10. On being bored and lost (in virtuality)
    Kristen Moore and Ehren Helmut Pflugfelder 152

Index 157

Notes on contributors

Denise Doyle has a background in fine art painting. Denise is an Artist Researcher, and Senior Lecturer in Digital Media at the University of Wolverhampton. Denise's research investigates the artist's experience in virtual worlds, and is developing a framework for a new theory of the Imagination that incorporates experiences of mediated spaces created through interdisciplinary research in Art and Technology. Her research interests include virtual worlds, philosophies of the imagination, practice-based research methods, phenomenological and ethnographic research methods, and multiplayer games and virtual learning environments.

Marcus Foth is Associate Professor and Principal Research Fellow with the Institute for Creative Industries and Innovation at Queensland University of Technology, Brisbane, Australia, and team leader of the Urban Informatics Research Group. His research explores human–computer interaction design and development at the intersection of people, place and technology, with a focus on urban informatics, locative media and mobile applications.

Norman Gough is Emeritus Professor at the University of Wolverhampton, UK, where he established research programmes in multimedia and computer games, and a distance learning instructor for the Laureate International and the University of Liverpool.

Ruth Greenaway is a former secondary school teacher with 15 years of experience whose teaching practices focussed on the development of innovative learning experiences for students, creating an excitement for learning. Ruth completed her Master of Learning Management in 2004. She was awarded an APAI scholarship for her PhD studies on 'School-Community Engagement: A Critical Approach to Involving Young People in Urban Planning'.

Justin B. Hollander is an Assistant Professor in the Department of Urban and Environmental Policy and Planning at Tufts University. His research interests are in the areas of public participation, brownfields reuse, shrinking cities, and land use planning. His work on public participation in planning is featured at www.open-neighborhood.org

Li Jin is a Senior Lecturer at the University of Westminster, UK. Her research is centred on cost-effective VR solutions for real-time interactive applications in the field of online education and cultural informatics.

NOTES ON CONTRIBUTORS

Vassilis Komis is an Associate Professor at the Department of Educational Sciences and Early Childhood Education at the University of Patras. His publications and research interests concern the teaching of computer science, the pupils' representations in the new information technologies and the representations formed during the use of computers in the classroom, the integration of computers in education, the design and the development of educational software.

Brian Magerko is an Assistant Professor in Digital Media in the School of Literature, Communication and Culture at the Georgia Institute of Technology. Dr. Magerko is the head of the Adaptive Digital Media (ADAM) Lab, which focuses on creating digital media experiences that alter themselves for pedagogical, dramatic, or entertainment gain for individual users. Dr. Magerko has published extensively in technical and design conferences on his work in creativity and cognition and the use of artificial intelligence and digital game environments for education and training.

Kerry Mallan is Professor in the School of Cultural and Language Studies in Education, Queensland University of Technology. Her research interests include children's literature, youth and new media, and narrative, with particular attention to feminist and queer theories and the relationship between youth and popular culture. Kerry has published extensively across literary studies, education, new technologies and popular culture.

Shailey Minocha, PhD, is a Reader in Computing in the Department of Computing at The Open University, UK. The focus of her research is understanding users' interactions with technology and investigating the socio-technical contexts in which computer systems operate. Shailey's recent research projects have involved investigating the role of social software and 3D virtual worlds in training and skills development with a particular attention to the virtual team-working, socialisation, collaborative learning and community-building capabilities of these tools.

Kristen Moore is a PhD candidate at Purdue University working on her dissertation research. Her place-based research focuses on public participation and technical and professional writing.

Ehren Helmut Pflugfelder is a PhD candidate in Rhetoric and Composition at Purdue University. His research focuses on digital rhetoric and technical communication, and his dissertation articulates a rhetoric of mobility and technology. He has published in *Composition Forum* and the *Journal of Sport & Social Issues*, among other outlets.

Ahmad John Reeves, PhD, is a Research Fellow in the Department of Computing at The Open University, UK. Ahmad's post-doctoral research position at the University of Bath focused on the role of identity in the design of Computer Mediated Communication (CMC) systems. He has also taught Human Computer Interaction at Kind Saud University, Saudi Arabia. His research interests include the use of linguistic models of participation to better understand what happens between people who interact through collaborative technologies, and how 'designed structures' are appropriated by the communities that form within them.

Pete Rive, the CEO and founder of LaunchSite, has been researching and working in virtual reality since 1999. He has 20 years experience in the screen industry and is

NOTES ON CONTRIBUTORS

Chair of Film Auckland. He is currently consulting with Education New Zealand and Clemenger BBDO on a virtual island in *Second Life*. He has consulted with Auckland City's Broadband Advisory group, the Auckland Metro's Innovation and Leadership group, and the KAREN networks advisory group. He is currently enrolled in a PhD studying knowledge exchange in *Second Life*.

David Thomas is a doctoral student in the College of Architecture and Planning at the University of Colorado. His area of research concerns the affects of digital media on environmental design, virtual spaces, and leisure places.

Aukje Thomassen is an Associate Professor and Research Director at Massey University's Institute for Communication Design in Wellington. Her research focuses on social innovation through design research (philosophy, didactics, and methodologies) and thereby studying knowledge creation in the creative industries (especially in the area of digital media/interaction design) within a theoretical framework of Cybernetics.

Iro Voulgari is a PhD candidate at the Department of Educational Sciences and Early Childhood Education at the University of Patras.

Zhigang Wen is a Business Development Engineer in Imagination Technologies, UK. His main research interests include real-time computer graphics, natural language processing for 3D animated virtual agents and automatic gesture generation.

Greg T. Young graduated in 2008 with a Bachelor of Creative Industries with a major in Communication Design from Queensland University of Technology. He received the award of a University Medal in recognition of an exceptionally high level of performance throughout his studies. Greg is now a freelance web developer and snowboard instructor.

Learning and researching in virtual worlds
Jeremy Hunsinger and Aleks Krotoski

The development process behind this book began as a special issue for the journal *Learning, Media, & Technology* half a decade ago. Aleks Krotoski and Jeremy Hunsinger were both PhD students at the time, in two different countries, both using Linden Labs' *Second Life* as a field of study. However, the pair quickly realised that they approached it in very different ways and with very different objectives: Aleks was tracking the flows of social influence through its online friendship networks, while Jeremy was investigating the politics of knowledge of the internet. Despite the differences in their lines of enquiry, through occasional encounters in person and online, they discovered several unanticipated crossovers between their work that stretched beyond the environment in which they set their academic activity. They realised that this digital community – and similar others – offered different things to different scholars, but there were commonalities they observed across both the learning and research fields that would be useful for people also exploring these spaces for fieldwork. Combining their common interests, they decided to bring together the growing body of practitioners who were flocking to this and other online environments in virtual and meatspace forums.

To explore the possibilities devised by this contemporary research community, Jeremy and Aleks created the *Learning and Research in Second Life* workshop series, supported by Linden Lab and held at Internet Research 8.0: Let's Play in Vancouver, Canada. John Lester, the Linden Lab Education liaison known within *Second Life* as Pathfinder Linden, supported the workshop in person by giving the keynote for the workshops. The series continues today, adapting to new technological functionalities and interests built upon the current literature, and Jeremy and Aleks have been honoured to offer the organisation responsibilities to the next generation of scholars who bring new perspectives. They would like to thank the participants, organisers or producers who have contributed to the discourse over the years, and whose work has been published in this volume.

Introduction

Virtual worlds are persistent, shared, online computer-mediated spaces where people collaborate to perform a wide variety of tasks. The environments can be 2- or 3-dimensional and can adhere to a limitless number of fantasies depending on the (personal or commercial) interests of the designers. The worlds that they comprise can be enclosed within the computerised environment, or they can become embedded in our everyday lives.

Over the last half century, various forms of virtual reality have progressed from fiction to fact. Digital spaces have evolved from early complex systems, like the CAVE automatic virtual environment and flight simulators running on mainframes that filled a room, to today's online virtual worlds and MMORPGs that can be accessed from a wide range of fixed and handheld machines. These virtual spaces have migrated slowly from deeply computerised and technologised environments of the 1960s and 1970s and their cybernetic imaginations into the commonplaces of our ubiquitous communication societies. Now, we use virtual worlds through personal computer systems and mobile devices, they are embedded within and upon our non-virtual space and in augmented realities and cognitive extensions. As we have become more familiar with these digital milieu, it has become apparent that they are a reflection of everyday life: the passions of their users, their interests, their practices, their thoughts, and their hobbies. As we increasingly embrace virtual worlds as places of work and play, they become more interesting as sites of learning and research, and demand closer inspection.

The most similar work to virtual worlds analyses has come from the group of academics that studies online communities. This area has a rich history that stretches back to McKenna & Green's theoretical analysis of virtual group dynamics (McKenna & Green, 2002) and has a precedent in the post-modern theories of non-physical community dynamics developed by sociologists in the late 20th century (e.g., Goffman, 1959). Our understanding of this area and the overlaps with virtual worlds work continues to evolve as new technologies are developed that feature richer communication facilities, from text to audio to video. The compendium of research and learning papers included in this volume are therefore a snapshot of the opportunities offered by the current crop of high-tech networked solutions for online communities to interact in virtual worlds.

What have evolved are opportunities for practitioners and researchers to explore these spaces as fields of expression of our everyday lives. They have advanced our capacities to interact in mediated spaces and offer new pathways to elaborate on existing practices. In addition, the mainstream adoption of new communication media over the last century has boosted the variety of methods that practitioners can integrate into their classrooms and research designs – both new and established. The rapid dissemination of technologies, practices and methods affords possibilities for distance teaching and learning, new study techniques, and unimagined research questions. Similarly, the limitations of these technologies require that practitioners adapt their practices to their benefits as well as their shortcomings.

Histories of virtual worlds

Although the technologies that we use today are attuned to the spaces and systems of their users, these environments have been part of the online collaborative storytelling landscape for decades.

The histories of virtual worlds derive from digital games and technological systems, and represent national cultural history and contemporary imaginations and realities. Their content and design has been inspired by and designed from many disciplines, including literature, sociology, anthropology, psychology, philosophy and folklore.

Regardless of the technologies that have run them throughout the decades, the stories in environments – and those used to legitimate them – are stories of the economy, of our society and our humanity.

This collection takes as its starting point that the history of virtual worlds is one of the messy intermingling between humans and machines[1]. It aims to emphasise that this history offers a scaffolding upon which we may build an understanding of how to learn from them, to learn in them, and to come to know the human condition more fully through them.

Over 300 English-speaking virtual worlds were recorded in 2009, and their prevalence in countries like China, South Korea and Japan indicates that the global number of virtual worlds is much higher. Their unique affordances offer opportunities that extend physical environments because they allow an immersive place in which to test impossibilities: within the virtual world, what can be real or treated as real is more than what is real in our physical worlds.

Additionally, teachers and researchers can trace the co-construction of realities amongst populations, allowing us to examine the development of shared histories that suffuse the learning and research agendas as they are imported into and emerge from the online space.

Researching virtual worlds

Although computer-mediated, virtual worlds are multifaceted social systems like the offline world, and choosing to study virtual world phenomena demands as much consideration for the participants, the environment and the researcher as any other research endeavor. Situating research in an online community demands reflexivity; as an immersive field of study, it demands more patience, self-awareness, and thoughtfulness toward research design than a lab-based experiment.

The mutability of the environment and the experiences within them – as close to or as far from reality as is possible within the constraints of the technology and the design – must to be taken into account when researching in virtual worlds. What appears at first to be a virtual world replica of an offline phenomenon may actually be subject to very different pressures and restrictions. Similarly, something that seems to be potentially very different from reality may be an extension of a commonly observed phenomenon in a different guise.

This raises the question of social and cultural understandings of research and the role of the contexts within our practice, and the relationship between researcher and researched. By placing our fieldwork in co-constructed, mediated environments, we must consider the modes of participation and engagement that are appropriate for this kind of space. It raises issues of the assumptions and research traditions at a deeper more reflexive level; the context may emerge as relevant or irrelevant in interesting and important ways.

As the chapters in this volume indicate, there is a thriving and considerate community of virtual world research keen to share best practice for methodologies through forums, seminars, focus groups and other events. There is less a hidden college and more an open and public collegium with which researchers can engage in order to conduct research in virtual worlds.

Virtual worlds as learning-centred environments

Virtual worlds are places where humans interact, and as such can be learning environments. However, as we have noted, they are complex and mutable in ways that more controlled and traditional environments are not. Thus we need to be more careful in our learning designs to account for these differences or perhaps to use the capacities of virtual worlds opportunistically. Four decades of eLearning practice and learning design research has demonstrated that simply reproducing experiences that exist in physical spaces can lower learning and research outcomes in comparison to designing specifically to take advantage of the affordances of the new environment.

Networked and non-networked computer systems have allowed practitioners to standardise learner-centred teaching practices in formal learning environments. They also create time and cost-saving simulations, and allow for nuanced and personalised opportunities negating any perceived loss of quality: extensive evidence suggests that using technology in courses either in a classroom or delivered at a distance has no significant difference in results than physical classroom environments (see http://nosignificantdifference.wcet.info/index.asp). In light of this, virtual worlds are having an impact on global educational policy, drawing attention to new possibilities for organising education outside formal environments of our current research and learning institutions.

Their interests likely stem from the pedagogical trends towards personalised learning strategies celebrated by education researchers. In particular, virtual worlds support socially-directed opportunities; and social learning in virtual worlds is almost unavoidable.

The genre of the software that has been most used by teachers and researchers as a field of study is the social virtual world, an environment that claims no overarching goal, as in game-based spaces, but provides a mediated environment simply as an articulated space for interpersonal interaction. The openness of the systems allows for the variety of objectives to be enacted in a way that doesn't conflict with a specific global aim. They provide natural arenas for group projects, shared exploration, shared knowledge building, dissemination, conversation and data collection. They often incorporate tools for building custom materials, which allows participants to engage with specified and controlled practical and experiential activities that fulfill the requirements of the learning and research programmes. Furthermore, there are unique opportunities for co-production of artifacts.

Global opportunities

Many virtual worlds have a global reach, providing access to not only materials for research and learning, but also active participants from different countries and cultures. The involvement of cross-disciplinary and cross-cultural participants can transform research projects. Although challenges that are apparent offline still arise online – linguistic, cultural, pedagogical, theoretical – the simplicity that the integrated virtual world environment offers practitioners and researchers the opportunity to work together in an incredibly rich medium. The challenge of internal institutional barriers related to work-life, disciplinary efforts, and interdisciplinary research and learning has been well documented elsewhere as has the possibility of transdisciplinary solutions to some of the problems (Hunsinger 2005; Hunsinger 2008).

Some of the most fruitful collaborations in virtual worlds are those that work transdisciplinarily. These collaborations bring many people together from a wide variety of fields to build and share ideas around the global problem they share. Two projects based in the virtual world *Second Life* that exemplify this are SciLands (see http://www.scilands.org/) and Info Island (see http://infoisland.org/). They represent large collaborations all seeking to explore issues and problems that unite various disciplines in one virtual world. They move beyond disciplinary interests toward the larger issues involved.

Conclusion

Despite the opportunities that these spaces offer, rich virtual environments demand creativity and labour in order to be robust spaces for learning and research. It is a challenge to be reflexive about the frames through which both learners and researchers engage with the digital world and one another, with the contexts of the learning and/or play, and the degree to which it is possible to elicit meaning based on the artifacts designed for the learning or research objectives. The differences, affordances, and constraints of these spaces will be part of what explains our insights or learning.

Virtual worlds are an evolution of social, networked, persistent systems. The research and learning endeavors that practitioners pursue in these spaces should reflect the large body of literature that has led to this point, and continues apace. Research organisations and association like Digra (Digital Games Research Association) and AoIR (Association of Internet Researchers) bring generations of researchers who work in virtual worlds and similar environments together to exchange knowledge and experience. Similarly, many conferences interested in pedagogy or internet research often have space for specialist groups interested in the web and virtual worlds. We encourage researchers to engage with the scholarship and research in the past and present when they engage with virtual worlds, as that will help to continue to develop and legitimise the fields of virtual worlds research and learning in virtual worlds.

This book draws together research papers from international practitioners who have identified alternative practices of learning and researching in virtual worlds. They deal with environments that break down borders of self-expression, creating spaces for play and expanding discourse in formal and informal settings. They focus on interactions that occur between the individual and the machine, between friends in social networks and between embodied avatars in new ways. They focus on process and outcomes and consider the new raft of questions that arise from engaging in teaching and research in these spaces, including new approaches to research ethics, internationalisation, localisation, and collaboration in virtual worlds. They cover a wide array of materials across many disciplines and interdisciplinary endeavours. We hope this book will be part of the dialogue in the ongoing evolution of this discipline.

Notes

1 For a closer look at the histories of virtual words see Ken Hillis's *Digital Sensations*, and Richard Bartle's *Designing Virtual Worlds*. For more on the history of virtual worlds research, see Ralph Schroeder's *Being There Together*.

References

Goffman, E. 1959. *The Presentation of Self in Everyday Life*. Edinburgh, UK: Anchor Books.

McKenna, K.Y.A & Green, A.S. 2002. Virtual Group Dynamics. *Group Dynamics: Theory, Research, and Practice*: Vol 6(1): 116 –127.

Hunsinger, J. 2005. Toward a Transdisciplinary Internet Research. *The Information Society* 21 (4): 277–79.

Hunsinger, J. 2008. The Virtual and Virtuality: Toward Dialogues of Transdisciplinarity. In *Exploring Virtuality Within and Beyond Organizations: Social, Global and Local Dimensions*, edited by Niki Panteli, and Mike Chiasson. London, UK: Palgrave Macmillan.

Immersed in Learning: supporting creative practice in virtual worlds

Denise Doyle

School of Art & Design, University of Wolverhampton, City Campus North, Molineux Street, Wolverhampton, WV1 1DT, UK

> The *Immersed in Learning* project began in 2007 to evaluate the use of 3D virtual worlds as a teaching and learning tool in undergraduate programmes in digital media at the University of Wolverhampton, UK. A question that the research set out to explore was what were the benefits of integrating 3D immersive learning with face-to-face learning for students who were already comfortable inhabiting the digital realm? The purchase and development of Kriti Island on the *Second Life* grid saw the online virtual space rapidly assume a sense of real presence, and become a focus for collaboration, nationally and internationally. The successful submission of the *Kritical Works in SL* project to the International Symposium for Electronic Arts (ISEA) in Singapore 2008 meant that Kriti Island hosted 10 international artists' work produced in and for *Second Life*, with a further exhibition, *Kritical Works in SL II*, launched at ISEA 2009 in Belfast. With the ongoing research new questions have emerged. There is now a deeper focus on the use of the *Second Life* platform for creative practice and the exploration of concepts that are impossible in real life. This article reflects on the development of an island for research and to support creative practice and creative collaboration and comments on its current and future use in the School of Art and Design.

Research context

Second Life, the online environment or 'virtual world' created by Linden Lab, was launched in 2003 with barely 1000 users (Rymaszewski et al. 2007, 5). The number of residents is now over 16 million, or at least those who hold a *Second Life* account.[1] The academic and teaching community were early in their recognition that a virtual world such as *Second Life* had many potential applications in teaching and learning. It developed out of the concept of the 'metaverse' described in *Snow Crash*, a novel by Neal Stephenson; the metaverse was meant to be a real place to its users, although it still relied on the real world as a metaphor. In July 2007, the University of Wolverhampton purchased an island on the *Second Life* grid to support research in the digital media area of the School of Art and Design and to encourage collaboration both within the institution and further afield.

The research presented in this article contributes to an emerging area of study in art and design educational research and its use of virtual worlds such as *Second Life*. The decision to buy the island in 2007 for a range of research purposes has, in itself, created further research questions and opportunities that could not have been anticipated at the time. As Kriti Island is coming to the end of its third year of 'presence' on the grid, discussions on the concepts of space and the notion of virtual 'place' have been possible with students and collaborators. The second phase of the *Immersed in Learning* project in 2009 was undertaken with undergraduate students in photography: firstly, to gather responses to the international work presented as part of the *Kritical Works in SL* exhibition, and secondly, to gather student perceptions of Kriti Island as a virtual space to develop creative practice. Interested students had the opportunity to take part in a virtual exhibition on the island later in the academic year.

Place in virtual worlds: creating Kriti

> There is no place in cyberspace – there's no Africa there, no mud, no beads or wells or such humanity in the very air. (Griffiths 2005, 269)

In *Virtually U*, Jenning and Collins (2008, 184) identify two types of virtual campuses being created on the *Second Life* platform: that of the Operative Virtual Campus, as illustrated by an island owned by INSEAD, and the Reflective Virtual Campus as illustrated by the archipelago of islands developed by Ohio University. The Operative Campus functions as a working campus, where learning, research and communication take place completely in a virtual environment that could not exist in the real world. In contrast, the Reflective Campus affirms the institutions' spirit and reproduces its physical campus in the virtual world.

In its initial development Kriti Island followed the Operative Virtual Campus model. Distinctly different from the University of Wolverhampton campus, Kriti Island is a place that, beyond the initial stage of development of a dramatic central landscape and welcome area, has evolved organically and by adaptation to use. The welcome area holds information about the island, the projects and the teaching and learning opportunities associated with Kriti. An amphitheatre area was developed close to the welcome area as a central point for presentations and viewing of video streams of student work. Other spaces have evolved over time, such as the social and meeting area, the library, and the seminar space, which will be discussed later in this article. Further to this, in the summer 2008 the island was used to house the *Kritical Works in SL* exhibition, and in summer 2009 the entire island was given over to the second phase of the exhibition.

The 'sense of place' that the island has assumed since its inception has been of particular note, with students and collaborators referring to Kriti as though it were a real place. Jones (2006, 12) notes that:

> The historical context of the use of imagined and experienced virtual spaces, as well as cyberpunk dream of making the cyberspace/matrix/Metaverse into a reality, frames the imagination of *Second Life*'s creators and users. In fact, *Second Life* takes the production of virtual spaces further by allowing the users to be gardeners themselves, landscaping their world as they wish it to be.

The use of the building, creating and landscaping tools of *Second Life* to sculpt, create and experience 3D space to test new concepts has formed the basis of the potential use for students in the area of digital media.

Creativity and practice in *Second Life*

The early use of virtual environments for artistic exploration has been well documented as a result of projects such as Art and Virtual Environments at the Banff Centre, Canada, in the early 1990s (Moser 1996). Perhaps it was inevitable that the artistic community would also move their creative practice to incorporate or explore virtual worlds as a new artistic space. However, little research currently exists on the use of virtual worlds in this context.

When researching the use of the *Second Life* platform for creative practice, a number of themes emerged, although of particular note was, whatever the mode of creative practice, the artistic focus on exploring what is clearly impossible 'In Real Life'. In conducting a survey of creative practice in *Second Life*, through work undertaken in the fields of art, media arts, architecture, performance and machinima,[2] I noted in particular the goals of the Ars Virtua Gallery[3] to be a laboratory for the formation of new art practices and to:

> [...] provide a platform for the intersection of media and the information/knowledge fields [...] to promote the development of a commons in networked space, a place where ideas can be exchanged across physical borders inside a shared experiential space.

The artist Lynn Hershman Leeson currently explores *Second Life* as an archiving space for her extensive projects created over the last four decades in performance, film and interactive installation called *Regenerative Presence: Documenting Life to the Second Power*. In 2007 Robbie Dingo, aka Rob Wright, re-created the 'space' of the painting *Starry Night* (1889) by Van Gogh on an entire island in *Second Life*. Also in 2007 Paul Sermon created

Liberate your Avatar (2007), a telematic project based on a protest by the Manchester-born suffragette, Emily Pankhurst, who at one time locked herself to the railings in the All Saints Gardens.

The performance artist Joseph DeLappe has incorporated online gaming into his work since 2001 and is well documented through *Dead_in_Iraq* (2006–ongoing) and *War Poets Online* (2004–ongoing). However, between March and April 2008 DeLappe re-enacted Salt March to Dandi in 1930 in *Second Life*, spending 26 days 'walking' through *Second Life* using a customised treadmill, which powered the movements of his InWorld counterpart. About *Salt March to Dandi* (2008) DeLappe (2008) writes:

> The original walk was made in protest of the British salt tax [...] for this performance I walked the entire 240 miles of the original march on a converted treadmill at Eyebeam in New York City and online in *Second Life*. My steps on the treadmill controlled the forward movement of my avatar, MGandhi Chakrabarti, enabling the live and virtual re-enactment of the march.

Why did DeLappe choose to re-enact an actual protest from 1930 in *Second Life*? Why did he choose to mediate it through the *Second Life* space? Perhaps the answer lies in the ability of DeLappe to assume the presence of Gandhi, through his avatar counterpart.

Another real-world artist, DC Spensley, known as DanCoyote Antonelli in *Second Life*, extends his artistic practice in *Second Life* into performance. Early in 2008 the author watched the second-only performance of *ZeroG Skydancers III* (2008), which is a group piece performed 'live' to a very small (virtual) audience at a cost of $3000L per seat.[4] This was an interesting decision, which according to DanCoyote, was an attempt to reflect the value of the time spent InWorld developing the costumes and the performance itself, yet appeared to be a large amount of money in the *Second Life* context. In this performance, the dancers' virtual bodies are abstracted, expanded and extended through magnificent and Impossible in Real Life costumes. This is an attempt at an immersive space that is, effectively, 'performed'. The audience are seated in an amphitheatre-styled area, and are passive, and not invited to participate. We set our view to mouse-lock and guide our viewpoint of the performed space.

Real life Australian artist Adam Nash, known as Adam Ramona in *Second Life*, has developed a substantial body of conceptual work in *Second Life* through an exploration of sound and immersive spaces. Of the interactive installation, or participatory artwork, *A Rose Heard at Dusk* (2007), Nash (2007) writes that the work:

> [...] is designed to be 'played' by visitors avatars. Walking, flying and jumping through the space, avatars create a unique audiovisual composition, different every time [...] visitors are actually playing the space like an audiovisual instrument, creating endless variations of sound and vision.

The colour saturated space of *A Rose Heard at Dusk* is motionless until you, or rather your avatar, moves through the installation itself.[5] Then, the space reacts to you, colours move and change and triggers sounds and changes of pitch. This piece, and many of his others, asks the avatar audience to explore the spaces he creates, as this is the only way to make the works come alive.

Each of these projects pushes the boundaries of the *Second Life* space with respect to extending creative practice. But in what ways are the works doing this? The project *Kritical Works in SL*[6] in 2008 aimed to bring together a range of art works to explore if common themes were emerging. Was there a commonality of approach and emergent experience? The artists that were invited to contribute to the *Kritical Works in SL* project were selected because they were already exploring the *Second Life* platform in some way in their creative practice, whether it was in the fields of art, design, media arts, virtual environments or sound technology. The aim was to include a diversity of practices and to encourage responses from a range of backgrounds. Some contributors are very well known within *Second Life*, or rather their virtual personas or counterparts are. The works presented in the exhibition contributed to the exploration of the potentials and limitations of the medium itself. What potentials in the works displayed could the students in Art and Design take, that could give them a new experience of their practice, or indeed, the presentation of their practice?

Kriti Island as a student exhibition space

In early 2009, as part of a Level 3 undergraduate module, Creative Industries and Opportunities, a group of photography students were invited to participate in presenting an existing photography exhibition of theirs, *Fact or Fiction* in a different context on Kriti Island. In Week 6 of the semester, during an introduction session to *Second Life*, each student had to set up a *Second Life* account, select their avatar type and find their way to Kriti Island for a photo-shoot (see Figure 1).

What was striking to me, after conducting a number of *Second Life* introductory sessions over the last two years, was that the students in digital media and the students in photography responded in very similar ways to the interface and to the space itself. In fact, surprisingly, there was really no difference between them. The first thing everyone wanted to do was to change their avatar, to be either closer to the way they look in real life, or to another kind of representation of themselves. Interestingly, one photography student had pink hair in real life, and she quickly changed her avatar's hair to the same colour. It was astonishing how quickly the students changed their avatar's clothes, and individualised the representation of themselves, and also how they adapted to the interface.

Once everyone had managed to work out the controls for their avatar, and learnt how to sit and fly, it became a good opportunity for the students to

Figure 1. The student avatars after less than an hour InWorld (2009). (*Second Life*, Linden Research, Inc., San Francisco, CA, USA.)

explore the potential of the space. The viewing controls in *Second Life* are of particular interest in terms of photography, and filmmaking, as it is possible to easily change your point of view (POV) from, for example, the first person to third person. You can also explore the space, as you can easily move the camera independently of your avatar. Essentially the POV and the viewing camera offer much potential for the exploration of film shots and photographic compositions (see Figure 2).

Figure 2. The photoshoot with the photography students (2009). (*Second Life*, Linden Research, Inc., San Francisco, CA, USA.)

Figure 3. The final *Fact or Fiction* exhibition (2009). (*Second Life*, Linden Research, Inc., San Francisco, CA, USA.)

The student exhibition, *Fact or Fiction*, held at the Herbert Gallery in 2008 in Coventry, UK, was a response to the Victoria & Albert exhibition held at the same gallery, *Something that I'll Never Really See*. As a group the students decided that they did not necessarily want to replicate any space in the physical world in *Second Life*, and it was the same for the exhibition on Kriti. Neither did they want to simply replicate the exhibition at the Herbert Gallery in terms of the curation and presentation. After we met for the session it was agreed that the exhibition would be held above the existing gallery, which was set up for the Kritical Works Exhibition for International Symposium for Electronic Art 2008 in Singapore. The final stages of the development of the exhibition can be seen in Figure 3.

It was interesting to see the work presented on Kriti and to experience the virtual exhibition presented alongside the students' final-year degree show exhibition in the Art and Design building at the University of Wolverhampton in the summer of 2009.

Kriti Island as a seminar space

The Undergraduate Digital Media Programme in the School of Art and Design at the University of Wolverhampton traditionally attracts c. 400 students across the three levels annually. There are five distinct pathways that make up the programme: Animation, Film and Video Production, Computer Games Design, Interactive Media and Digital Arts and Media. Kriti Island was introduced to the students at each level of the programme. However, in 2008 there was a particular focus on the introduction of *Second Life* into two modules: a contextual module at Level 1 undertaken by all students in the division and a specialist Animation module, Character and Environment, at Level 2. I focus here on the use of *Second Life* as a seminar space to support the Level 1 contextual module.

All students registered at Level 1 studied the 15-week contextual module Understanding New Media. The module registration in 2008 was 140 students. The module structure relies on a one-hour lecture session for the whole group followed or preceded by a two-hour seminar session exploring and discussing ideas developed in the lecture. In the seminar the students work with pathway-specific staff with a maximum of 30 students per group. In Week 1, during the module introduction, the students were introduced to *Second Life*. They were encouraged to create an account and an avatar ready to participate in an online session later in the module. In Week 9 it was possible to have a face-to-face seminar session in a computer room with two of the seminar groups, Interactive Media and Computer Games Design students, which had *Second Life* installed on all computers. This enabled the whole group to support each other in the creation of their avatar and journey through Orientation Island, which is the first place that avatars find themselves once they have created an account. From student feedback, they were surprised by how much they enjoyed the session, particularly those who had not created a *Second Life* account until that day.

In Week 10 the students had the opportunity to participate in an InWorld seminar which was offered twice during the week, outside of the normal lecture slot. The seminar, 'Representing Reality: Synthetic Realism and the Film Image' was adapted from a lecture given during the 2007 lecture series of the same module. The content of the lecture lent itself to the experience of 'being' in *Second Life* as questions of how we both represent and experience reality were explored and debated. In March 2008 the author attended a presentation given by Simon Bignell at the MML08: Massively Multi User Workshop at Anglia Ruskin University in Cambridge, England.[7] The possibility of using a virtual world such as *Second Life* for simulation or simulation-based scenarios is evident, and in fact, Boston (in Aldrich 2005, 334), suggests that simulation-based environments are 'ideal for developing an understanding of big ideas and concepts – those things that experience alone can deepen understanding'. During his presentation Bignell most notably discussed the benefits of using the 3D nature of the user experience to explore and explain concepts. I wanted to apply some of his ideas to the development of the session on Representing Reality (see Figure 4).

The 2006/2007 session was structured around three images, each representing reality in different ways. It was my intention to allow the students to vote for which image, in their view, represented reality the most in the context of our discussion by adding a note card to one of three boxes. After the initial introduction to the session we discussed the text written by Manovich (2001) seen in Figure 4. The Manovich premise is that we have become so accustomed to the photographic image as an accepted representation of reality that

Figure 4. Preparation for the InWorld seminar (2008). (*Second Life*, Linden Research, Inc., San Francisco, CA, USA.)

what we attempt to do is to recreate something that is actually based on a film image and not on our actual experience of reality.

Following a discussion of the three videos/films that the images were from, a Chris Cunningham music video for Bjork, *All is Full of Love* (1999); *Polar Express* (2004) and *Grasshopper* (2005) by Richard Linklater, we discussed the Japanese Roboticist Mori's diagram of the Uncanny Valley (see Figures 4 and 5). None of the students who participated in the seminars had heard of the Uncanny Valley, although all of them seemed to grasp the concept very quickly.

Each of the sessions generally lasted one hour. In terms of participation there were proportionately more Computer Games and Interactive Media students who participated in the seminar. This may be accounted for by the fact that the other students studying Animation and Film and Video Production were not given the opportunity of a face-to-face session to set up their account in *Second Life*. Feedback from the students about the seminar session was generally positive and all students felt that the experience had been engaging, although most students tended to anticipate that this would be a one-off experience. I am uncertain as to what had created this perception.

Conclusions

In her review of games-based learning, De Freitas (2006, 52) notes that:

> ... learning in the context of immersive worlds is beginning to have more wide ranging uses and applications ... as Second Life communities demonstrate, *interactions within and between groups are opening up new opportunities for*

Figure 5. The group discussing Mori's Uncanny Valley (2008). (*Second Life*, Linden Research, Inc., San Francisco, CA, USA.)

learning beyond the classroom confines (physically and conceptually). [My emphasis]

Since 2007, the presence of Kriti Island has enabled a number of projects and experiments to be explored in the School of Art and Design. The activities undertaken for the *Immersed in Learning* project, the virtual exhibition for the photography students, and the immersive seminar exploring concepts of the Uncanny Valley taking advantage of the 3D nature of the *Second Life* space, both create new opportunities for learning in new contexts both physically and conceptually. Initially intended for digital media students, the interest in staging a virtual exhibition came from an area more used to exhibiting as part of the subject expectation itself, and the potential for students' creative practice extended through Jones' (2006, 12) gardeners concept, 'landscaping the world as they wish it to be', seems evident. Being able to create a space for international collaboration through the *Kritical Works in SL* exhibition also encouraged undergraduate students to explore and experiment on the *Second Life* platform further. A distinct disadvantage of developing practical projects for digital media students in *Second Life* was the necessity to develop a whole new set of skills that may not necessarily be able to be used on other platforms and scenarios. Already grappling with a range of other software expectations, this remains an issue in the further integration of the platform into the undergraduate programme.

Although research into the experience of being an avatar is not a focus of this study and is outside of the direct scope of the projects presented here, consideration of the interactive and immersive experience of the student is crucial to the overall understanding of the potential future integration of the *Second Life* space of Kriti Island into the digital media curriculum. As Meadows

(2008, 16) suggests, 'an avatar is a social creature, dancing on the border between fact and fiction'. The border he refers to has a rich potential for the exploration of character within animation and digital media, and may point to future directions in art and design educational research and application in virtual worlds.

Notes

1. Statistics from http://secondlife.com/whatis/economy_stats.php (accessed January 2, 2009).
2. The term 'Machinima' is used to denote video captured 'in' the virtual or game world.
3. Information accessed InWorld and available at http://arsvirtua.com/about.php (accessed April 14, 2008).
4. This is an approximate cost of $11 based on the Linden dollar rate on 5 October 2008. http://secondlife.com/whatis/economy-market.php. Linden dollars translate into real world money and have a value of approximately 270 Linden dollars to a single American dollar.
5. An account of the relationship between art works in *Second Life* and the use of the avatar for represented presence in virtual space is explored further in Doyle (2008a).
6. A catalogue was published of the final exhibition (Doyle 2008b).
7. The presentations were filmed and are available at http://www.inspire.anglia.ac.uk/mml08

References

Aldrich, C. 2005. *Learning by doing: A comprehensive guide to simulations, computer games, and pedagogy in e-learning and other educational experiences.* San Francisco: Pfeiffer.
Anon. 2008. *Ars virtua gallery mission statement.* http://arsvirtua.com/about.php (accessed February 10, 2008).
De Freitas, S. 2006. *Learning in immersive worlds.* Bristol: Joint Information Systems Committee. http://www.jisc.ac.uk/eli_outcomes.html
Delappe, J. 2008. *Tourists and travellers exhibition.* http://saltmarchsecondlife.wordpress.com/ (accessed July 3, 2008).
Doyle, D. 2008a. Art and the avatar: The Kritical Works in SL project. *Journal of Performance Art and Digital Media* 4, nos. 2–3: 137–53.
Doyle, D. 2008b. *Kritical Works in SL* (exhibition catalogue). Morrisville, NC: Lulu Publishing.
Griffiths, J. 2005. *A sideways look at time.* New York: Penguin.
Jenning, N., and C. Collins. 2008. Virtual or Virtually U: Educational institutions in second life. *International Journal of Social Sciences* 2: 180–6.
Jones, D.E. 2006. I, avatar: Constructions of self and place in second life and the technological imagination. *Gnovis, Journal of Communication, Culture and Technology* 6: 1–32.
Linden Lab. 2003. *Second Life.* San Francisco: Linden Lab.
Manovich, L. 2001. *The language of new media.* Cambridge, MA: MIT Press.

Meadows, M.S. 2008. *I, avatar: The culture and consequences of having a second life*. Berkeley, CA: New Riders.
Moser, M., ed. 1996. *Immersed in technology: Art and virtual environments*. Cambridge, MA: MIT Press.
Nash, A. 2007. *A Rose Heard at Dusk*. http://yamanakanash.net/secondlife/rose_heard_at_dusk.html (accessed February 10, 2008).
Rymaszewski, M., W.J. Au, M. Wallace, C. Winters, C. Ondrejka, and B. Batstone-Cunningham. 2007. *Second Life: The official guide*. Indianapolis, IN: Wiley.

Design of learning spaces in 3D virtual worlds: an empirical investigation of *Second Life*

Shailey Minocha and Ahmad John Reeves

Centre for Research in Computing, The Open University, Walton Hall, Milton Keynes MK7 6AA, UK

Second Life (SL) is a three-dimensional (3D) virtual world, and educational institutions are adopting SL to support their teaching and learning. Although the question of how 3D learning spaces should be designed to support student learning and engagement has been raised among SL educators and designers, there is hardly any guidance or research in this area. In this article, we report an empirical study in which we have elicited educators', designers' and students' perceptions of learning spaces within SL. Based on this empirical research, we have presented some design considerations for SL educators and designers who are involved in designing learning activities and spaces in SL. We hope that the design guidance and examples described in this article will support educators and designers to design learning spaces that foster students' socialisation, informal learning, collaboration and creativity.

Introduction

A three-dimensional (3D) virtual world (VW), also called a synthetic world, is a synchronous, persistent multi-user virtual environment, facilitated by networked computers, in which people, represented as avatars, experience others as being present in the same environment, or 'being there together' even though they are geographically distributed. 3D VWs support communication and collaboration more effectively than two-dimensional (2D) web-based environments by extending the users' ability to use traditional communication cues of face-to-face interactions in a way that 2D environments do not (Bronack et al. 2008; Eschenbrenner, Nah, and Siau 2008). In 3D VWs, users synchronously interact in 3D spaces via their avatars and converse in real time through gestures and audio- and text-based (chat and instant messaging) communication (Meadows 2008).

Second Life (SL) is the most popular 3D VW in the education domain. A wide variety of well-known educational institutions are using SL for a range of purposes, including distance education, presentations and meetings, historical recreations, literature and language acquisition. SL, unlike 3D games such as *World of Warcraft*, does not have a storyline or plot of actors and events. The lack of a guiding narrative in SL provides flexibility for educators to design learning spaces for their pedagogical requirements. Educators can design the learning space for the pedagogy, rather than the other way around, as in some off-the-shelf 2D virtual learning environments (VLEs).

An island of an institution in SL can provide a dedicated environment for learning, which helps to ensure a sense of belonging and purpose for the students. Clark and Maher (2001) analysed the role of 'place' in virtual environments which provides the basis for four key processes fundamental to a constructivist learning environment: context (meaningful and authentic), construction (of knowledge), collaboration and conversation (between students and educator(s) and among students): 'Selecting a virtual world as the technology for a virtual learning environment provides the basis for a place, but the place itself needs to be designed. The design of the place can be influenced by architectural design' (Clark and Maher 2001, 7). A 3D VW can provide students with a sense of place and context, where they are able to build and share their learning experiences.

As with the design of physical learning spaces (Oblinger 2006), the design of learning spaces in 3D VWs should be a representation of an educator's or institution's vision for learning. There are several models of 3D learning spaces. These range from replicas of real-life (RL) buildings and spaces, perhaps with the look and feel of a real campus, to the extremes of creating imaginary or fantasy locations (Prasolova-Forland, Sourin, and Sourina 2006; Jennings and Collins 2007).

There is, however, a lack of clarity about what creates a 'sense of place', and how 'place' is distinct from 'space' (Harrison and Dourish 1996; Dourish 2006). There is, also, no discussion in the literature on the impact of realism or fantasy elements of VW learning spaces on learning experience and the relationship between 'sense of place', design of learning spaces, and student engagement and experience.

There is little published research on the design and evaluation of learning spaces in 3D VWs. Therefore, when institutions aspire to create learning spaces in SL, there are few studies or guidelines to inform them except for individual case studies (e.g., Lucia et al. 2009). In a Joint Information Systems Committee (JISC)-funded research project called DELVE (**DE**sign of **L**earning Spaces in 3D **V**irtual **E**nvironments), we conducted an empirical study involving SL educators, designers and students to investigate their experiences with and perceptions of learning space designs in SL, and which key characteristics of learning space designs were important to them.

In this article, we report a study in which we have elicited educators', designers' and students' perceptions of learning spaces within SL. Based on this empirical research, we have derived some design considerations which, along with vignettes presented in the article, will provide useful guidance and triggers for ideas for educators and designers who are involved in designing learning activities and spaces in SL. Although we have focused on SL in our empirical study, we hope that the results will be applicable to other configurable 3D VWs.

Aim of the study

Our key research question (RQ) is: 'How should 3D learning spaces be designed for student engagement?' Three of the five subquestions of the DELVE project and relevant to the empirical research in this article are as follows:

- RQ1: What is meant by a 'learning space' in SL? Does a learning space mean a designated teaching area, or does learning also occur in sandboxes and social spaces?
- RQ2: How does the pedagogy influence the design of learning spaces, and vice versa?
- RQ3: Does the level of visual realism of a learning space influence the experiences of a learning activity, and why? In other words, given that SL offers a wide range of design possibilities, what do we gain or lose by incorporating visual realism in learning space designs?

Data and methodology

Our research methodology consisted of an online survey which was conducted at the start of the project involving colleagues from the further education (FE) and higher education (HE) communities and semi-structured interviews, guided by our RQs, with designers, educators and students. The various stages of our empirical research are described below.

The first stage of our research was to develop and conduct an online survey using the *Survey Monkey* (http://www.surveymonkey.com/) application. The purpose of the survey was twofold. First, we wanted to ask a range of questions relating to the design of learning spaces in SL from colleagues in the FE and HE community. Second, we wanted to invite the participants (who completed the survey) if they would be willing to take part in a short follow-up interview. We received 46 filled-in questionnaires and 27 respondents expressed their willingness to participate in an interview.

In parallel with conducting the survey, we developed our research materials such as a consent form, project summary sheet, initial information request form or pre-interview questionnaire, and interview templates for students, educators and designers. The educators' and designers' questions related to aspects such as the description of the learning spaces, factors affecting designs, levels of realism, learning activities and any modifications they had made to the spaces in response to feedback and their experiences. The students' questions covered similar issues along with emphasis on the design aspects that either supported or hindered their experiences. These research materials were submitted to the Ethics Committee of our institution for approval prior to carrying out the interviews.

In addition to recruitment via the survey, other modes of participant recruitment were: notices in some of the education groups within SL and personal invitations to colleagues. Ahead of an interview, we sent the project summary sheet and the consent form to the participant. The participant was encouraged to ask questions of us (the research team) while they were looking at the materials. We already had details of the islands and activities of the survey participants from the survey data but to all the other participants (who had not participated in the survey) we sent a pre-interview questionnaire. Although we had generic interview templates for each category of the participants, some participant-specific questions were added to each of the interview templates based on the information we had about the participant either from the pre-interview questionnaire or from the survey data or any other resources (websites, blogs, papers, reports) that the participants had alerted us to ahead of the interview.

In all, we interviewed seven students, 10 designers and 22 educators. Four interviews were conducted over the phone while 35 interviews were conducted in SL. Some of the educators in our set of participants were also designers or had influenced the designs of the learning spaces in SL and some of them had even built the spaces but in our interviews with educators, we focused on questions from an educator's perspective. The phone interviews were audio-recorded, and transcripts of text-based SL interviews were saved into individual files.

Our RQs (listed above) provided the lens to analyse the data from the participants. An inductive or thematic analysis of the data was undertaken by the project team to identify the themes, subthemes and any causal or interrelationships between the themes for each of the questions (Braun and Clarke 2006). The inductive analysis involved two team members of the research team independently reading the interviews. After an independent data analysis among the coders, the team focused on finding recurring themes in the analysed data.

In this article, we report the data analysis from the core subset of the data. For each of the derived themes, vignettes (quotes) from the interviews are included. Each quote is an excerpt from the data and is associated with the participant type (e.g., designer, student, educator). From each of the theme and subthemes in the analysed data, we have derived design considerations or design principles for designing learning spaces in SL. These design principles are consolidated in Table 1 in the 'Implications of our research' section of the article.

Main findings of the study

Interpretation of learning spaces in Second Life

This theme relates to the educators' varied interpretations of a learning space in SL (RQ1). For example, some of the educators mentioned that a learning space could be where a formal, educator-led learning task occurred, or where students had the opportunity to socialise with other students, or where the students could interact with resources. Alternatively, a learning space could be islands in SL, other than the institution's island.

Indoor and outdoor learning spaces

The first distinction we can make is in relation to whether the activity takes place 'indoors', i.e., in some structure or building or 'outdoors' in an unenclosed space of some sort. Some educators described learning taking place 'indoors' and in spaces similar to RL, for example:

> We have an in-house auditorium as opposed to an open air amphitheatre type of facility – I think the consensus is to have the amphitheatre kind ... although having all the people seating here has some advantages ... at Harvard they like to have their learners in a circle outside so everybody can see each other and gestures, but that can be distracting for some kinds of events, having all the avatars all facing forwards not distracting each other could have some advantages. (Educator, see Figure 1)

Figure 1. University lecture theatre (*Second Life*, Linden Research, Inc., San Francisco, CA, USA).

Figure 2. Formal classroom setting (*Second Life*, Linden Research, Inc., San Francisco, CA, USA).

In the lecture theatre there is normally a narrow corridor entrance, which means that avatars could feel crowded into a small space, making the movement difficult (see Figure 1). One educator in our data-set designed a classroom to allow for more space for access and between the seats (see Figure 2):

> Let me show you my classroom. It's completely off-the-shelf rather than the way I wanted it. It's easier to navigate and get in and out and stand on your seats here than the auditorium, it's better here. (Educator)

Some educators perceived indoor spaces as providing a sense of delineation from other spaces and also some level of privacy for the learning activity. Indoor spaces were also perceived as supporting formality and authority relationships between educators and students similar to traditional learning environments:

> I think it [enclosed spaces] can work. Traditional learning anyway, after all we hold normal face-to-face tutorials in rooms. We don't want the students to wander. (Educator)

Some educators described their learning spaces as being 'outdoors':

> I've used the tree platform on *SchomeBase* [name of an island], the tree platform on *Open Life* [name of an island]. I've built a 'chessboard room' which was put in the sky above the teaching and learning space on *Open Life*. (Educator)

> We also have a little garden which we use for tutorials and orientation. (Designer)
>
> Visually I tried to make it look like a place that's been situated in a park. Things like trees and things like grass, walkways ... so in that sense it's consistent with what you would see if you wandered around a physical space. (Educator)

Indoor versus outdoors could be dependent upon the subject being taught, for example, science and literature, in indoor and outdoor spaces, respectively:

> Well indoors is ok for science seminars and practical too for the boards and diagrams. (Student)
>
> Probably outside near trees with wooden benches ... to bring out the inner self for literature ... relaxing. (Student)

However, some spaces, indoors or outdoors, can induce reactions of fear of falling or being drowned and claustrophobia in the users similar to those in RL:

> All hated the room which was completely closed, two students were claustrophobic in real life, and really didn't like that room. We actually abandoned the session and went to the tree house. Just taking the roof off that room, made it okay. It's got to make students feel comfortable. I say that because of my experiences with the claustrophobia. (Educator)
>
> There are interesting observations about people identifying so strongly with their avatar that they feel actively stressed and frightened when 'they' fall in water, or get lost, or stuck in some strange space. (Educator)

Real-world-like settings for users new to Second Life

One reason that the educators gave for choosing RL-like learning spaces was to provide a familiar environment to students who are new to SL, or to relate to the users' expectations and mental models from RL:

> I've heard that people who first come into *Second Life* expect something traditional: normal offices, normal chairs and humanoid avatars. People who have been in SL for a while like something innovative. Unusual settings, animal avatars, etc. Because most of my small group of students were new to SL, and were coming just for the tutorials, I wanted to be traditional ... and I wore this avatar you see, with a suit and tie. (Educator)
>
> Things like chairs do have a purpose in structuring meetings and discussions and giving social signals that people can recognise, same with the buildings. (Educator)

Open spaces and sandboxes for students new to Second Life, for socialisation and building/scripting activities

Moving in open spaces can be easy and comfortable for users who are new to SL and who are learning to control their avatar's movement:

Figure 3. Sandbox area (*Second Life*, Linden Research, Inc., San Francisco, CA, USA).

> Well, I think that for newbies it is a good idea to be on land in an open space so people don't fall down or get trapped … so it could be up in the sky or underwater if that's where you have a clear space. (Educator)

Participants also mentioned how open spaces and sandboxes on an island facilitate students learning from one another (see Figure 3 for an example of a sandbox). In a sandbox, students can practise their SL building (programming) skills in a setting similar to an RL design or arts workshop or studio, view each other's artefacts and share their experiences:

> I have also seen people working in the sandbox and helping each other so that is another way I see learning happening. (Designer)

> I think, from a design point of view, it should be an open area to allow for freedom of movement and expression. (Student)

> The programming class actually meets in the sandbox and to practise scripting. (Designer)

Activity-focused learning spaces
Educators mentioned giving guidance to students about where the learning was expected to occur and they felt that a larger SL space could be intimidating or confusing for learners without some form of spatial delineation and/or

referencing as to where learners needed to be and what they were expected to do:

> I think there needs to be a designated place for a class but this could be anywhere. I think students can't deal with the whole space. Each learning scenario works if it is task-orientated. Students obviously would need to know where to be and what is expected of them. (Educator)

> We created a large building for their creative arts faculty, principally for their fashion students so that they could stage fashion shows there, invite SL fashion designers in to talk about their work, and also let the students set up shops so that they could sell their own fashions so as to get to understand the commercial side of running a fashion business. (Designer)

As research in the physiological aspects of learning has revealed that active engagement with the learning objects – whether a lecture, laboratory process, text or creative medium – increases the likelihood that the learner will both retain and be able to use information and skills later (Zull 2002). One educator in our data-set expressed in a similar vein that learning takes place where the resources are:

> Normally the learning takes place in the point of contact with the resources. (Educator)

Learning space is the entire island

Even though specific areas in an island are designated for learning, our participants perceived the entire island as a learning space, as the island provides opportunities for chance encounters, informal learning and socialisation. In fact, the de-centredness of the architecture emphasises the principles of socio-constructivism (Felix 2005) where the whole campus or island is perceived as a learning space for co-learning and co-construction of knowledge rather than emphasising classrooms (Grummon 2009):

> The whole island – some places are used more than others, and there are areas that are designated for learning and where you would expect it to happen, like the bit with the chairs and the presentation board, but people bump into each other and start talking and developing ideas, etc., at any point on the island and because of the social nature of SL. I think this sort of social constructivist learning is very relevant whether it was designed or spontaneous. (Designer)

Learning can happen anywhere in Second Life

Our participants utilise a wide range of places in SL to send their students out on tours, activities and exploratory assignments. They view the whole of SL as a learning space, not just one particular area or island:

> Any space you come to can be a learning space, it just depends on your topic. Stores and malls can be teaching places for maths, advertising, management, you get the idea. (Designer)

> The instructional design class meets here [island of the university] and then goes out [within SL] to find educational sites and then return [to the island] to discuss their findings. (Designer)

> The whole ethos was that nearly everything we do is learning as learning doesn't just happen in formal set contexts. Living is learning and becoming part of a community and developing your identity is learning so it's happening everywhere. (Educator)

Relationship between the pedagogy and design of learning spaces

This theme relates to the RQ2 in which we investigated how the pedagogical underpinnings and learning activities influence the design of learning spaces and vice versa.

Pedagogy and design of spaces influence one another

For some educators, the design of the spaces has been guided by the learning activities:

> I would say pedagogy first, without discussions about pedagogy, what we mean by this at Surrey, we can't hold meaningful conversations with staff who are unfamiliar with the environment and we don't think the students will benefit either. (Educator)

In contrast to the standard didactic instructional approach, other educators mentioned that, for the design of 3D spaces, SL can support experiential or active learning, that is, learning through doing and reflection, or by role-playing. For example, an arts and design educator said:

> The pedagogy. We are basically doing what we have always done in art education. Providing a studio space for the creation of things, with lots of discussion around the creations. It is easier and cheaper in many ways in a virtual world to do this, so *Second Life* is like a hyper-studio ... It resonates very strongly with our educational philosophy. ... It [SL] is good for experiential learning. (Educator)

> Pedagogy definitely – my philosophy is to use the tool that suits the need not find a need to fit the tool just because you have it. The aim is that the students use the space ... Make sure the activities are authentic and useful to the students – the wow factor of being able to fly is not sufficient to keep them engaged if they can't see the purpose in using the space. (Educator)

However, some of our participants felt that it was not necessary for the pedagogy to drive the designs of learning spaces but to first understand the possibilities that SL provides:

> I find the political correctness of 'pedagogy must lead technology' to be rather sterile. We need to be more interactionist about this. The teachers don't know what is possible [in SL], and the technologists don't know what the teachers might want to achieve if they could. So, to try to answer the question: about what we might [emphasis] be able to do to inform the ideas about what we might want [emphasis] to do. (Educator)

Some of the participants mentioned how, for them, it was first a case of understanding what SL's affordances are and what SL can provide as a learning environment, and then designing the learning activities:

> I think that it should be the pedagogy that comes first, though in my case its interactive, I look at what SL is and then I design pedagogical approaches to use it so maybe SL comes first in terms of the constraints and opportunities of SL, and the opportunities are out in the world there, not necessarily on my island. (Educator)

> Yes, with my particular classes I had to see what was possible [in SL] first and then adapt. We have a lot of hands on content that can't always be conveyed in a traditional lecture. (Educator)

The flexibility of SL allows alternative approaches to the designs of spaces to be organised easily to match the pedagogical requirements and students' experiences. For example, the designs of learning spaces could easily be adapted to match the learning activity by accessing objects from the user's inventory in SL in real time and laying them out on the island (provided the user has the access rights to do so):

> I'm not sure it was pedagogy, it was first trying to understand how virtual spaces work, so the notion that if you want an activity you don't need a dedicated space that's always set aside for that activity you can pull something out of your inventory when you need it and put it away when finished. (Educator)

An educator, as well as the designer of her own island, discussed how she created some learning areas but left some open spaces on the island to see how the island would be used by students and educators. She then iteratively designed the island based on her observations:

> Bits of both [pedagogy and design] ... the thing that provided the magic hook for me was the community stuff, and that is what I wanted to enable, but I left open spaces and some deliberately ambiguous landscaping so that the island could continue to develop according to how people wanted or needed to use it. (Designer)

Visual realism in learning spaces

The following analysis relates to RQ3 on how the level of visual realism of a learning space influences designs of learning spaces and activities.

Visual realism for 3D simulations and visualisations

For some of our participants, there was a clear link between the level of visual realism and the effect on learning. For example, the high level of visual realism supported the teaching of particular subjects, like history (see Figure 4):

> So if you have an island that teaches Mexican history, e.g., Mayan architecture you can definitely get students to experience the Mayan culture by playing the role of explorer in ways they've never been able to do before. They might have been able to do it, but with huge cost. Everything virtual prior to *Second Life* was accompanied by huge cost. Now you can bring that environment to every desk, every teacher, any classroom with hardly any cost at all. (Educator)

The flexibility of designing 3D objects and realistic simulations in SL enables learning that would not be possible otherwise. For example, an educator discussed photo-realism with regard to the design of an object within the learning space (a computer motherboard, in this example):

> The things I teach are obviously based on real life, but being able to walk on a [computer] motherboard gives the students an opportunity to talk about specifics which in real life are just small bits on a board. (Educator)

The ease and flexibility of building objects in SL also enables students to build objects and learn by doing and visualising:

> Because you can do things so easily, i.e., access and build and shape materials, i.e., wind turbines, for many of my students they wouldn't be able to make one in real life, but in SL they did it in a couple of classes. So it allows them to

Figure 4. Visit Mexico (*Second Life*, Linden Research, Inc., San Francisco, CA, USA).

explore the potential to make things in a virtual way, it gives them confidence to say I could make one in RL. (Educator)

There is a place in SL called the sacred temple of geometry and they have lots of models of geometric shapes, etc., which I think are a great aid to learning! (Student)

A student discussed her experiences of attending an astronomy seminar in SL (see Figure 5):

Well, at a talk on supernovas, all the audience were able to zoom in on the presenter, then he could fly around different parts of the inside of the night-sky sphere he had built. It was very effective and certainly something that you would not see in real life, and this was happening seemingly all around you. Yes, immersive is the word, and it felt like being on a personal tour of the sky. (Student)

Well, SL is a very good place to do immersive teaching, the more a student becomes involved in what he/she is doing the more apt they are to learn on a deeper level. (Designer)

Flexibility is one of the key elements in the design of physical learning spaces (Oblinger 2006). It should be possible to quickly reconfigure the learning spaces to support different kinds of learning activity – moveable chairs and tables, for example. In SL, the flexibility of designing spaces is not constrained to moving the furniture but the entire environment and the scenery of the learning spaces can be changed. For example, the learning space can be made realistic or non-realistic to match the topic being discussed. A student

Figure 5. An astronomy seminar (*Second Life*, Linden Research, Inc., San Francisco, CA, USA).

Figure 6. Philosophy debates (*Second Life*, Linden Research, Inc., San Francisco, CA, USA).

participant who leads a philosophy discussion group in SL gave some examples (see Figure 6):

> Changing the scenery each week has definitely added a dimension of interest for a lot of people. If you look over to the northeast, you'll see a large head like thing – I made this for the topic 'Consciousness' and I asked members to add items that they felt were things that go on in people's minds. The purpose of this was to get people involved. Another would be the 'Just War' topic where I set up a war scene, complete with invading aliens.

The student reflected on the relationship between the design of spaces (realistic or non-realistic) in SL, the discipline of philosophy and the learning experience:

> I do think the atmosphere makes a difference. It's key because it shows that we are serious about philosophy and this is not just a general chat space. Atmosphere equals setting up an interesting environment that is relative to the topic – it absolutely does 'feel' more engaging. I think people got the idea straight away. It became a sort of thing you expected in our debates, a sort of signature for the event.

Realism for familiarity and comfort to the user
Visual realism was often used to provide familiarity and support learners' existing mental models of what to expect (Lakoff and Johnson 2003; Bronack et al. 2008) and how to interact or behave:

> I think having visual realism helps people feel comfortable with the environment, and if they are comfortable then you can extend the boundaries of the activities a bit further. When I canvassed input from all the people I know who use SL regularly before I developed the islands there were one or two who said it should be totally fantastical and that is the point of SL. For them, it works. In my experience they are in a very small minority and most other people need to feel connected to real-world visuals in order to feel comfortable. (Designer)

Visual realism in the designs of spaces gave students 'clues' about how to make sense of the environment and how to interact with the environment as these quotes show:

> I have given this a lot of thought – students need certain reference points when they are entering an unfamiliar space. For example, we created definite pathways through the exhibition and some signposts and a welcome message but after that it is up to the student to explore. (Educator)

> The context of a realistic environment will give students a starting point and guide them. So they may build houses that are on the ground and in lines – whereas a whacky landscape with floating buildings will give them different ideas. (Educator)

> It can definitely affect how you behave, for example, when you enter this building, you may want to sit on chairs even though you don't need to, but on a psychological level would you feel more tired or less relaxed if you were having a conversation mid-air. Some level of visual realism provides clues to a person on how they might behave. (Educator)

Visual realism or non-realism is learning activity- and context-dependent

This example highlights the relationship between realism or non-realism in designs of spaces and the intended learning:

> But it depends what you're doing. So with Hadrian's wall, that was trying to be as accurate as possible with them trying to work out how high this wall should be and they were dressed up in Roman costumes and they had to run around between the wall and the ditches to see how high the wall should be in order to defend it properly. So realism was very important there; we asked them what does it feel like trying to defend the wall given the height that it was set to. So the immersive reality was very important there. (Educator)

In addition to the three key themes (directed by our three subquestions RQ1, RQ2 and RQ3), we encountered various social, organisational and pedagogical factors that influence designs of learning spaces which we discuss in the following two subsections.

Designs of learning spaces within an island

Combining formal learning areas with social spaces to encourage informal learning

In real-world situations, while formal learning normally occurs in pre-designated places, informal learning can take place anywhere, or in what Jay Cross terms 'learnscapes':

> Informal learning is the unofficial, unscheduled, impromptu way people learn to do their jobs. […] Formal learning takes place in classrooms; informal learning happens in learnscapes; that is, a learning ecology. It's learning without borders. (Cross 2007, 15, 237)

Although critics say that it is impossible to formalise informal learning, Cross maintains that the key to informal learning is to optimise learning outcomes, or provide the opportunities:

> What I want to do is optimize learning outcomes. Optimization means removing obstacles, seeding communities, increasing bandwidth, encouraging conversation, and so forth. (Cross 2007, 237)

It is clear from our data that learning in SL can occur in a diverse range of spaces, and not just within designated learning spaces and set up by the educators. Social spaces on the island encourage socialisation and informal learning through observations, interactions and collaborations.

Some educators consciously chose to have 'formal' aspects of their learning spaces, sometimes described as 'study areas', 'classrooms' or 'libraries', etc.:

> And to the left is the study area, it's a sort of more formal area, with various buildings, a big exhibition centre which allows students to display their work, there are also social spaces [bar on the beach, dance area]. (Educator)

Educators and designers suggested that SL enables both asynchronous and synchronous learning, and, therefore, the learning spaces should be designed to facilitate individual learning as well as learning with fellow students.

Spaces for asynchronous learning

SL can support asynchronous activities as SL has 24-hour access as opposed to the restricted access to physical classrooms:

> SL has helped change some aspects … it [SL] is more likely to get the students to do more leaning on their own. (Educator)

> We have the ability in here to create spaces where students can work asynchronously. For instance my tutorial on appearance that I believe is still laid out in the sandbox could be used on a student's own time. Where in a college classroom you do not have access to the classroom after hours because someone else is using it or it is locked. (Educator)

> My students can use that space to have synchronous discussions and use some of the materials in the building asynchronously. (Educator)

> I also see students working outside of class time, and I see evidence that they have been working the next day when I look at the island and see what has changed. (Educator)

Designing for socialisation, collaboration and community building

Instead of designing lecture theatres and auditoriums where students watch the educators perform, the designers of physical learning spaces are being challenged to create learning environments that facilitate collaborative activities such as flexible meeting places (Oblinger 2006). In our study, students and designers discussed how the design of learning spaces in SL could facilitate socialisation, collaborative learning and community building, for example, having communal spaces such as cafes with comfortable seating areas around formal learning spaces.

A student of Marlboro College, Vermont, discussed how dedicated platforms in the sky for student projects promoted student interactions and socialisation:

> The project spaces (elevated platforms) that she [the educator] places for our use in the latter half of the course invited people to look at and interact with each other's work. My friend and I were neighbours on the highest platform, and we talked a lot, sharing in both class-related and non-class discussions. (Student)

Designers discussed how the spaces should be designed to exploit the affordances of SL such as avatar-based interactions, navigation in 3D spaces and synchronous communications to encourage chance encounters, social interactions and enable community building:

> It [design] should encourage and enhance social interaction and possibilities both through planned and accidental avatar interactions and also through the creation of a space with a unique visual identity that can be owned by the community of users, to enhance that sense of community. (Designer)

> I think it is important to remember that SL for learning is primarily about collaboration between people via their avatars – our in-world design should be geared to support that. (Designer)

The authority of the educator and social norms

Some of the participants commented on the spatial designs related to authority within a learning space. Seating arrangements can imply a power relationship; having a facilitator positioned higher up on a podium infers singular authority, whereas having an educator sitting at the same level in a circular arrangement infers shared and collaborative authority:

Do you have the facilitator standing on a podium, looking down on the students ... or sitting in a circle where everyone is equal? I think almost every thing that applies to real-world sessions applies in here. People designing learning spaces should keep that in mind. (Designer)

Placement of seating areas and awareness of how people use the space helps to make that a more efficient process. If people [avatars] are too far apart, they do have less of a sense of engagement, however, 90% of the effectiveness [of a session], I have found, is in establishing an atmosphere. (Student)

Formal and informal seating arrangements to suit the activity

There were mixed views from the students in our data-set about the formal and informal seating arrangements within the learning spaces. While some students preferred the relaxed nature of informal settings such as circular seating areas on stools and boxes rather than chairs (see Figure 7), one student remarked how the informal seating arrangement could encourage relaxed one-to-one conversations among the students rather than focused and serious discussions:

It is much more relaxed to have a circular seating area, feels more personal I suppose, not one person at the front and everyone else looking at them, more like participating. (Student)

And structure ... proper chairs, not beanbags, for example ... it should look more formal ... not necessarily like a classroom with desks and chairs but not like somewhere people would go to just to 'hang out' ... I've noticed that [in]

Figure 7. Informal seating arrangement (*Second Life*, Linden Research, Inc., San Francisco, CA, USA).

group discussions where it's been a circle of bright colourful beanbags, the discussion tends to quite quickly break down because everyone is relaxed and starts chatting in IM (instant messaging), etc., but when discussions [are] more structured, people sitting on chairs in a room, that doesn't happen, the concentration seems to stay on the discussion. (Student)

Some educators also felt that there was no relationship between the formality or informality of the design space in SL and student learning. In fact, some of them have deliberately chosen informal and relaxed settings for making the learning environment novel and engaging for the students:

Do our students learn less because they are a little more relaxed in what feels like an informal environment here than if they were in some stuffy, formal, lecture theatre with me at the front of the class using *PowerPoint* slides and talking AT them, I don't think so. I think they learn more in an environment as informal as this one, they learn more when relaxed, informal, their tutor is playing with their own identity and there are butterflies flying about and they have a cup of tea in their hand. (Educator)

We have thrown out the proverbial desks. And populated the space with wikis and blogs and chat rooms. And the same is true here. Students don't need to be close enough to a teacher to see or hear in the usual way, because our cameras can zoom. We can use our workspace differently than we would a desk. We can chat with our team members who are across the sim or even on a different sim, or with *Sloodle* those who are not even in SL. And we need to think in this way to be able to use the world as a classroom or learning space. The SL world and also the ever flattening real world. (Educator)

Designers suggested being creative in using objects in the design of spaces that invoke fun, playfulness and student engagement:

Playfulness engages. Engaged learners are more likely to retain what they have learned especially if it challenged their mindsets or surprised them, so in answer to your question, that's the reason why I like to be creative with my environments, like the applecart teleport point that greets visitors when they go near it; no one expects an apple cart to act as a teleport, let alone talk to you. (Designer)

One of the educators mentioned whether or not learning takes place is context dependent and factors, similar to RL, such as a student's concentration, the educator's preparation and student's expectations determine student learning and engagement:

The learning takes place wherever the student's mind is at the time. The place where the avatar is can be distracting or facilitating. It depends on context. (Educator)

Er, for me it's not really realism that is important. It's the student's reaction to the space. The experience for them rather than the virtual environment. This has to do with things such as their expectations, the tutor's preparation and a whole host of factors. The realism of the build is just icing on the cake. Often the most realistic sims are the most empty. (Educator)

Designing to provide affordance

Affordance is a property in which the characteristics of an object or environment influence its function (Stone et al. 2005). In other words, what the learning space is for, or the purpose of the objects, should be clear from their designs:

> It needs to be very clear what the aim of the space is, it should be really really [emphasis] very clear and that should not be because there is a nice sign saying what it is for but it should be in the character of the development. Something in the look and feel, the way you interact with the space is representative of its use so that will make it easy for the user to understand. (Educator)

Co-designing learning spaces with students

In several data-sets in our study, educators mentioned involving students in the design of learning spaces to encourage a participatory design approach where students create design solutions. Engaging the students in the design process also facilitates team working, fosters creativity and community building:

> It should encourage exploration and creativity – students are more likely to engage if they are able to engage in the creation of the space and not be presented with a finished environment where they have no control. I think it should encourage interaction with others and social learning. (Educator)

Ambience and aesthetics of the learning space

Ambience and visual aesthetics are important design criteria for the design of learning spaces as they are perceived as ways to engage students:

> They liked the way the birds sang, and the daylight changed to evening as we sat there. (Educator)

> If they feel relaxed here – from visual stimulation, or aural (sound of water flowing) – or whatever reason, then maybe they engage more with the tutorial and say more than they would in real life in a lecture hall or for something comparable with MSc usage – they are distance learners and we use discussion boards, *Skype*, wikis, blogs, email, and so forth. (Educator)

Design of learning spaces to avoid interruptions

The Open University (OU) in the UK initially had one island (*Open Life*) in SL which had a mix of social and learning spaces. However, due to interruptions to tutorials from other students or visitors who were primarily involved in social activities, the OU now has a second island (*OUtopia*) with social spaces such as a village pub, beach, beach huts and houses:

> When the halls were on Open Life there were always students hanging around and they started to crash the formal tutorials. (Educator)

Some other universities (e.g., Georgia State University, Atlanta) have also built more than one island (and sometimes closed one of the islands to the public) for research or specifically for teaching:

> We built a small school and the researcher will be studying teacher anxiety, students will role-play kindergarten students and one will be teacher. We are using that island to ensure that the [research] study is not inadvertently interrupted. (Designer)

Some educators have set up access controls for certain areas on an island:

> We have access controls here if needed where only MScers [MSc students] are allowed on land although we have never 'flipped the switch'; it's good to know it's there if needed. (Educator)

Some other educators have designed spaces in the sky or on elevated platforms to avoid interruptions:

> The advantage of the two places I built myself was I could place them in the sky, it made them private. (Educator)

> Well, the Kira Cafe is very conventional I suppose, there are two rooms, one a large social area, and a second area more removed from casual passers-by. I have found that having casual people just dropping in on meetings can be very disruptive. (Student)

Implications of our research

In our data, we have noted that educators and designers are clearly taking advantage of the 3D features of SL and its interactivity and flexibility for designing (and re-designing). SL designers and educators are adopting a user-centred design approach: trying out designs, evaluating them with students and then re-designing and improving the designs based on the feedback. Therefore, the designs of learning spaces are changing and evolving through this iterative user-centred design and evaluation process.

Here are some questions that educators and designers may ask when designing for 3D learning spaces, interactions and objects: Are students expected to work on a task within a space? Where will the resources and objects for that task be situated? Will students be involved in building and scripting? Will students be involved in the design of learning spaces? Will students work in teams? How should the learning spaces be designed to support both formal activities and providing social spaces for informal learning?

Based on the design considerations and vignettes presented in this article, some principles for the design of 3D learning spaces are proposed in Table 1.

Table 1. Design principles for 3D learning spaces.

Theme or subtheme	Related design principles
Interpretations of learning spaces in SL	• Consider indoor spaces such as auditoriums and lecture theatres to support formality and authority relationships similar to traditional learning spaces in RL • Avoid designing spaces that could potentially trigger phobic reaction or do not provide an easy exit • When designing outdoor spaces, consider the issues of privacy, interruptions from visitors and possible distractions for users (e.g., sounds of water flowing or the sound of the wind) • The discipline of the learning activity could guide the choice between outdoor and indoor learning spaces • Consider the SL skills and backgrounds of the users while designing learning spaces • Design RL-like learning spaces for users who are new to SL and 3D environments • Design activity-focused learning spaces to make it easier for students who are new to SL to understand the activity and what is expected from them • Consider open spaces and sandboxes for imparting programming skills and to enable the students to learn from one another • Do not be constrained by the learning resources and spaces in your own island. Explore other islands in SL for learning resources, for student induction, to gain awareness of SL's potential, to conduct virtual field trips with students, and for networking with other SL residents
Relationship between the pedagogy and the design of learning spaces	• The learning activity and any underlying pedagogical underpinning (e.g., experiential, instructional) should guide the design of the learning spaces • Design learning activities that exploit the affordances of SL for education (such as synchronous communication, 3D simulations and visualisations, and so on) • Exploit the flexibility and ease of bringing out objects from the inventory to set up learning spaces in real time in SL to match the learning activity • Design learning spaces iteratively to match both the users' requirements and feedback, and how the existing learning spaces are being used
Visual realism and non-realism in the design of spaces and activities	• While considering the visual and non-visual realism in the design of objects in the learning spaces, or the design of learning spaces themselves, take into account the learning activity and the discipline • Visual realism can help to recreate historical simulations and visualisations that may be difficult to replicate in labs in RL such as models of solar systems or wind turbines • Consider visual realism in the designs of spaces and activities to provide familiarity and comfort to users who are new to SL

Table 1. (*Continued*).

Theme or subtheme	Related design principles
Design of learning spaces within an island	• Design an island with spaces that facilitate both formal and informal learning • Design learning spaces for asynchronous learning • Design for socialisation, collaboration and community building by integrating formal and social spaces, providing large workshop/studio-like areas for students to work on projects • Design spaces to match the educator's authority that needs to be represented; for example, a podium for the educator or a circular seating arrangement for informal discussions and to allow for peer-to-peer exchanges • Consider formal or informal seating arrangements for the students to match the learning activity • Design spaces by choosing unusual objects that invoke fun and engagement • To articulate the aim of the learning space, choose objects in the design of the space that match their intended function and purpose • Consider co-designing learning spaces with students as a way to teach them SL programming skills (e.g., in a design course or a computer science course) and also to enhance their sense of engagement with SL and the learning spaces • Consider the ambience and aesthetics of the designs to make it engaging for students • Consider setting up access controls on learning spaces within an island to avoid interruptions • Design learning spaces in the sky or an elevated platforms for privacy and to avoid interruptions

Examples of the principles can be found in the vignettes discussed above. These design principles should provide useful guidance and triggers for ideas to educators and designers who are planning to set up learning activities and spaces in SL. (The 'user' in Table 1 refers to SL educators and students.)

Conclusions

Instead of replicating traditional instructional delivery modes such as seminars and lectures, learning spaces in SL are being utilised to foster creativity among students, aid socialisation, facilitate informal learning and enable exploratory and experiential learning rather than traditional instructional ones. Therefore, there is a transition from the traditional 'directional' mode of teaching to a more social constructivist pedagogy. The social constructivist approach emphasises the socially and culturally situated context of cognition, in which knowledge is constructed in shared endeavours (Duffy and Cunningham 1996;

Felix 2005). Further, through role-play scenarios and simulations, students are getting opportunities to practise work-based skills such as remote team working, communication and collaboration in distributed geographical work settings.

Our research in the DELVE project has shown that designs of learning spaces in SL were perceived by those interviewed to influence student learning and engagement. However, there are several contextual factors that may impact on student experience such as students' SL skills, their motivation and educators' SL skills and preparations for the activities, whether SL is a compulsory component of the programme, whether SL activities will be assessed, and nature of delivery on the course or programme (distance education, face-to-face, or blended delivery).

Therefore, creating a learning space in SL is only a part of the process of creating a sense of 'learning and teaching place' in SL (please refer to the 'Introduction' section of this article where we introduced the concepts of 'space' and 'place'). Also, 'Space is the opportunity; place is the understood reality' (Harrison and Dourish 1996, 67). In other words, educators can create the learning spaces, but it is the students that create the places through their usage of that space. This is another reason why many educators in SL are allowing their students to have a major stake in creating the space as well. They reasoned that if students can contribute to creating the type of space they want, it will become the type of place they want to learn in (Wahlstedt, Pekkola, and Niemela 2008; Whitworth 2008).

Limitations of our empirical investigations

We were only able to gain the views of a limited number of students compared with educators and designers in our empirical research. More input from students might have given us a clearer insight into any specific learning-related considerations from their perspective. Further there is a need to conduct longitudinal studies where we can capture users' experiences over a period of time. This would enhance our understanding of the interrelationships between learning experiences and the designs of the learning space in 3D VWS as the designs evolve over time. Another key limitation is that we have not (to date) evaluated the design considerations proposed in this article. We plan to introduce the design considerations to SL educators and designers and ask for their feedback on applicability and usefulness of the design considerations.

Taking this research further

There are two key areas that we are currently investigating and which we hope will contribute towards a better understanding of the design of learning spaces in 3D VWs. We will report these aspects in our future publications.

Influence of the designs of physical learning spaces and vice versa

The design of physical learning spaces has a direct impact on the learning that takes place within them (Oblinger 2006). For the design of learning spaces in 3D VWs, it is useful to draw out lessons from the design of physical learning spaces. On the other hand, a 3D VW can provide a cost-effective prototyping environment to develop models or simulations of physical learning spaces and to evaluate the stakeholders' interactions and experiences with these simulations. These evaluations might provide insights into how the spaces being envisaged would be used in the real world and the improvements or changes could be made to the designs (e.g., The Acklam Grange School case study [*Teaching 4 Learning* 2009]).

Principles of game usability and universal design

Research is needed to make 3D VWs more accessible and usable. In addition to the usability principles of flexibility, affordance, designing for ambience, which we have discussed, there is a need to refer to studies in games usability (e.g., Isbister and Schaffer 2008) where heuristic evaluations (evaluations against design heuristics or principles; see Stone et al. 2005) are conducted to evaluate the fun, flow, playfulness, choreography and engagement of games. The principles of game usability and accessibility or universal design (e.g., Lidwell, Holden, and Butler 2003) will help enrich the designer's toolbox for designing and evaluating 3D learning spaces.

Investigating the applicability of the findings in this article to other 3D VWs

It will also be worth exploring the applicability of the design considerations, derived and presented in this article, to other 3D VWs. The determining factor will be the level of configurability available to designers or developers in other 3D VWs. For example, 3D VWs such as *Open Sim* or *HiPiHi* are, like SL, highly configurable by users, whereas others such as *Habbo Hotel* or *Gaia Online* have much more limited user content creation and environment manipulation possibilities.

Acknowledgements

The research presented in this article has been supported by JISC's Learning and Teaching Innovation Grant (July 2008–June 2009), Faculty of Mathematics, Computing and Technology at The Open University, UK, and the Teaching Fellowship (January 2008–December 2009) from Centre for Open Learning of Mathematics, Science, Computing and Technology, one of the Centres for Excellence in Teaching and Learning at The Open University, UK. We are grateful to David Kernohan, JISC programme manager, for his support and encouragement, Dr Karen Kear at The Open University, UK, and to Dr Nick Mount and his team at University of Nottingham, UK, with whom we have collaborated on the DELVE project. We would like to express our sincere thanks to the participants in our study for their time and insights.

References

Braun, V., and V. Clarke. 2006. Using thematic analysis in psychology. *Qualitative Research in Psychology* 3: 77–101.

Bronack, S.C., A.L. Cheney, R.E. Riedl, and J.H. Tashner. 2008. Designing virtual worlds to facilitate meaningful communication: Issues, considerations and lessons learned. *Technical Communication* 55, no. 3: 261–9.

Clark, S., and L. Maher. 2001. The role of place in designing a learner centred virtual learning environment. In *Computer aided architectural design futures*, ed. B. de Vries, J. van Leeuwen, and H. Achten, 187–200. Dordrecht: Kluwer Academic.

Cross, J. 2007. *Informal learning: Rediscovering the natural pathways that inspire innovation and performance.* San Francisco: Pfeiffer/Wiley.

Dourish, P. 2006. Re-space-ing place: Place and space ten years on. In *Proceedings of the ACM conference on computer supported cooperative work*, 299–308. New York: ACM Press.

Duffy, T.M., and D.J. Cunningham. 1996. Constructivism: Implications for the design and delivery of instruction. In *Handbook of research for educational communications and technology*, ed. D.H. Jonassen, 170–98. New York: Simon & Schuster Macmillan.

Eschenbrenner, B., F.F.-H. Nah, and K. Siau. 2008. 3-D virtual worlds in education: Applications, benefits, issues and opportunities. *Journal of Database Management* 19, no. 4: 91–110.

Felix, U. 2005. E-learning pedagogy in the third millennium: The need for combining social and cognitive. *ReCALL* 17, no. 1: 85–100.

Grummon, P.T.H. 2009. Best practices in learning space design: Engaging users. *EDUCAUSE Quarterly* 32, no. 1. http://www.educause.edu/EDUCAUSE+Quarterly/EDUCAUSEQuarterlyMagazineVolum/BestPracticesinLearningSpaceDe/163860.

Harrison, S., and P. Dourish. 1996. Re-place-ing space: The roles of space and place in collaborative systems. In *Proceedings of CSCW'96*, 67–76. New York: ACM Press.

Isbister, K., and N. Schaffer. 2008. *Game usability: Advice from the experts for advancing the player experience.* San Francisco: Morgan Kaufmann.

Jennings, N., and C. Collins. 2007. Virtual or Virtually U: Educational institutions in Second Life. *International Journal of Social Sciences* 2, no. 3: 180–6.

Lakoff, G., and M. Johnson. 2003. *Metaphors we live by.* Chicago: University of Chicago Press.

Lidwell, W., K. Holden, and J. Butler. 2003. *Universal principles of design.* Beverly, MA: Rockport.

Lucia, A.D., R. Francesse, I. Passero, and G. Tortora. 2009. Development and evaluation of a virtual campus on Second Life: The case of SecondDMI. *Computers & Education* 52, no. 1: 220–33.

Meadows, M.S. 2008. *I, avatar: The culture and consequences of having a Second Life*. Berkeley, CA: New Riders.

Oblinger, D. 2006. *Learning spaces*. London: EDUCAUSE.

Prasolova-Forland, E., A. Sourin, and O. Sourina. 2006. Cybercampuses: Design issues and future directions. *The Visual Computer* 22, no. 12: 1015–28.

Stone, D., C. Jarrett, M. Woodroffe, and S. Minocha. 2005. *User interface design and evaluation*. San Francisco: Morgan Kaufman.

Teaching 4 Learning. 2009. Building a virtual school. *Teaching 4 Learning: The online magazine for all involved in education* March–April: 25–7. http://www.teaching4learning.com.

Wahlstedt, A., S. Pekkola, and M. Niemela. 2008. From e-learning space to e-learning place. *British Journal of Educational Technology* 39, no. 6: 1020–30.

Whitworth, A. 2008. The organisation of space and place: A commentary on Wahlstedt et al. *British Journal of Education Technology* 39, no. 6: 1031–6.

Zull, J. 2002. *The art of changing the brain: Enriching the practice of teaching by exploring the biology of learning*. Sterling, VA: Stylus.

Social virtual worlds for technology-enhanced learning on an augmented learning platform

Li Jin[a], Zhigang Wen[b] and Norman Gough[c]

[a]School of Electronics and Computer Science, University of Westminster, London, UK; [b]Imagination Technologies Ltd., Hertfordshire, UK; [c]School of Computing and Information Technology, University of Wolverhampton, UK

Virtual worlds have been linked with e-learning applications to create virtual learning environments (VLEs) for the past decade. However, while they can support many educational activities that extend both traditional on-campus teaching and distance learning, they are used primarily for learning content generated and managed by instructors. With the evolution of internet technology, social virtual worlds (SVWs) are now able to facilitate more social interaction, efficient visual communication, integration of rich media and sharing of student-generated content. They offer the prospect of lively interactive virtual communities in which users interact through their emotional avatars in a 3D virtual world. SVWs are being increasingly embedded into e-commerce and e-learning, and challenge our ideas about the next generation of VLEs. This article outlines the impact of emerging social networking technologies on the internet, reveals the convergence between social networking and virtual worlds for technology-enhanced learning (TEL), and examines the way in which SVWs are transforming the nature of learning as a social practice. The design and implementation of an innovative social interactive learning platform is presented, which augments SVWs and other social networking services with conventional learning management and student support systems. Practical experiments are described that have been prototyped on this platform, including e-tutoring and student-led exhibitions. The results demonstrate that an SVW can greatly enhance student-centred active learning experience on the augmented learning platform in comparison to traditional VLEs. It is shown that the platform has the potential to support both formal and informal learning, as well as facilitating social interaction, self-motivation, active engagement and creative thinking in TEL.

Introduction

A virtual world is a computer-simulated environment that users can explore, inhabit and interact with via avatars, which are graphical representations of the users. Due to the great impact of internet technology in the field of education, a virtual world as a powerful virtual reality-based medium for teaching and learning has been coupled with e-learning applications to be used as a virtual learning environment (VLE) for the past decade (Cunha, Raposo, and Fuks 2008; Hendaoui, Limayem, and Tompson 2008). Preliminary research indicates that virtual worlds support various types of educational activities as an extension to both traditional on-campus teaching and distance learning (Hetherington et al. 2008). However, conventional virtual worlds primarily support learning content to be generated and managed by instructors. Traditional e-learning applications rely on a mainly text-based asynchronous format to deliver learning materials to students. Such a passive learning approach lacks mechanisms to encourage creative thinking, social interaction and collaboration in educational activities. It is recognised that social and collaborative experience plays an important role in education (Araujo et al. 2007; Marsick and Watkins 2001). With increasingly pervasive high-speed networking connections and the evolution of internet technology, more social web-based applications are becoming available to support real-time three-dimensional (3D) graphics and rich media integration over the internet. Virtual worlds are evolving into social networked virtual environments, which provide interactive 3D environments accessed by multiple users through an online interface, while facilitating social interaction, efficient visual communication, integration of rich media and the sharing of user-generated content in a collaborative environment. Social virtual worlds (SVWs) as 3D social networking services are increasingly embedded into e-business and e-learning. For example, some well-known companies such as *Toyota*, *Dell*, *IBM* and the *British Broadcasting Corporation* (*BBC*) have begun to embed SVWs into e-commerce services and e-performance programmes. SVWs are also growing rapidly in popularity due to their game-play features and have become particularly attractive to the younger generation. As one of the emerging technologies, SVWs have expanded and challenged ideas for the next generation of VLEs. Researchers point out that it is important for educators to analyse SVWs in order to understand what the characteristics of twenty-first century learners are and how their learning is changing as a result participating in these environments (Breslin and Decker 2007; Churchill and Halverson 2005). This article first outlines the impact of the emerging social networking technologies on the internet and reveals the convergence between social networking and virtual worlds for technology-enhanced learning (TEL). It goes on to discuss the design and implementation of an innovative social interactive learning platform, which is intended to augment SVWs with conventional VLEs for supporting both formal and informal learning.

The impact of the emerging technology: social networking on the internet

In both professional and personal lives, various groups and communities based on affinities, expertise, age and gender are formed organically in order to work together and share goals. Not surprisingly, there is a significant inclination to migrate social networks to the online domain. With the rapid evolution of internet technology, the new generation internet is able to provide a two-way mechanism for users, which allows them not only to read and download content in a top-down approach as before but also to write and upload online content in a bottom-up approach. In conjunction with rich media and user friendly interfaces (Garrett 2009), it encourages users as producers to enrich information, including video, audio and even 3D data, by their comments and revisions. This stands in contrast to traditional internet use, which limits users to browsing content that only the site owner can modify in a top-down approach. The internet is being transformed into a platform for connecting people rather than a primary information repository and this has resulted in the development of social networking services such as *MySpace*, *Facebook*, wikis and blogs.

Being a novel social media for mass communication, social networking on the internet emphasises social interaction and share of user-generated content in a collaborative environment. Different social networking services focus on different aspects of human interaction (Weaver and Morrison 2008). For example, *MySpace* (www.myspace.com) allows self-publishing within the users' network of friends and colleagues. It is a media-based social network through using videos, movies, instant messages, news, blogs, etc. *Facebook* (www.facebook.com) is a peer-relationship-based social network that allows users to create personal profiles and build up social relationships with other users by uploading various media such as photos and videos. It aims to expand audiences, promote upcoming events and give users a feeling of belonging. A wiki provides a web-based collaborative interface for multiple users to co-edit content and add links. Blogs support regular and frequent content editing through the rapid posting of thoughts and images and interaction with the public through comments and responses. *YouTube* (www.youtube.com) as an online video-sharing network allows users to upload videos and share movie clips. It is regarded as the people's interactive television network, which allows contributors to share user-generated content with facilities for others to respond and comment.

The convergence between social networking and virtual worlds: social virtual worlds

It is observed that most social networking services on the internet are still heavily based on text, image and video such as blogs, wikis, *Facebook* and *YouTube*. There is a lack of efficient ways to support natural interaction that mainly relies on human sensory channels to handle perception, cognition and non-verbal behaviours such as gesture, posture and expression in real time. With the convergence of social networking and virtual worlds, the internet has already begun to foster an intuitive and immersive 3D SVW to address these deficiencies.

Social virtual worlds are intended to build up lively interactive virtual communities, which represent part of reality but also leave some space for fantasy to be incorporated. Users interact and communicate with each other through their emotional avatars in a 3D virtual world. One of the most successful SVWs is *Second Life* (www.secondlife.com) (Cliburn and Gross 2009; Kumar et al. 2008), an online social space in which users can explore, meet others, socialise and participate in individual and group activities for educational or business purposes. Since its introduction to the public in 2003, the 3D virtual community has grown explosively and today is inhabited by millions of users from all around the world. Some well-known companies have started to embed SVWs into their e-commerce services and e-performance programmes. They establish virtual branches in *Second Life* not only for promoting upcoming events and advertising new products but also for selling real products and services. For example, *Toyota* set up the product launch of the Scion xB in *Second life* which is aimed at the younger market (http://video.google.com.au/videoplay?docid=-3443834733977158362&q=second+life). A virtual car model can be dropped onto potential customers in a virtual world so that they can customise it. Visitors to the *Dell* virtual island in *Second Life* can sit at one of several drafting tables to configure their notebooks. *Dell* eventually wants to let customers purchase real PCs in this novel way (Dell 2009). The *BBC* staged its annual 'One Big Weekend' rock concert in *Second Life*. Online audiences were able to see avatars of their favourite musicians, as well as watch and listen to live streams of the bands on stage in Scotland. It is agreed that such SVWs added a new level of interactivity for those who were unable to attend physically (Salomon 2007). Furthermore, as a result of the popularity and success of massively multiplayer online role-playing games (MMORPGs), SVWs are rapidly growing in popularity due to their game-play features. These massive 3D virtual environments have been widely accepted by a wide range of people and they are particularly attractive for the younger generation. Millions of users spend hours at a time in SVWs socialising, competing and – most of all – learning, for example, learning how to build digital creative content (e.g., architecture and product), learning how to work as a team, learning how to make decisions and learning how to solve problems. They enjoy engaging with learning activities and are highly motivated and stimulated by these environments. Consequently, SVWs provide a significant new opportunity for promoting edutainment by learning through playing.

While offering a source of entertainment for users, SVWs also make a huge contribution to the users' active learning. They have begun to be used in e-learning by many institutions, such as colleges, universities, libraries and government entities. The National Aeronautics and Space Administration (NASA) set up a Collaborative Space Exploration Laboratory (Colab) in *Second Life* for people interested in space travel and technology (NASA 2009). The National Oceanographic and Atmospheric Administration (NOAA) built a number of fully interactive educational demonstrations on weather and ocean (NOAA 2009). Institutions explore SVWs for a wide range of educational activities including learning, teaching and research in order to enhance personal development skills within a collaborative and sharing virtual environment (Hetherington et al. 2008). Researchers and educators favour the innovative learning environment because it is more personal and social than traditional online learning (Hendaoui, Limayem, and Tompson 2008). Recently, *Second Life* has become one of the cutting-edge virtual learning platforms for major colleges and universities, including the University of Florida, Princeton, Harvard, Edinburgh University and Ohio University. For example, Edinburgh University in the UK runs distance learning courses with the aid of SVWs, including an M.Sc. in e-learning, M.Sc. in design and digital media and M.Sc. in entrepreneurship. *Second Life* is used as a social space for students and tutors to gather and meet. The feedback obtained from students is positive, especially about the 'learning as socially grounded' aspects of the course (Edinburgh 2009). The social advantages of a distance learning course employing SVWs are seen be attractive and potentially valuable to students when compared to conventional e-learning.

Social virtual worlds as learning environments: transforming learning as social practice

Due to the significant impact of a convergence between social networking and virtual worlds, SVWs are transforming the nature of learning as a social practice in a collaborative environment. SVWs not only allow users with specific learning requirements to be able to access and share learning materials from dispersed locations through an interactive online interface but also offer the following innovative characteristics of a social learning platform:

(1) Massive connections in shared 3D environments: to enable a large number of learners to connect together in shared 3D environments and be able to attract new learners.
(2) Multimodal interaction in real time: to provide learners with multiple modes of interaction through the internet including voice chatting, instant messaging (IM), etc.
(3) Self-organised socialisation and collaboration: to permit and encourage the formation of in-world social groups in order to coordinate and act together for shared or common learning objectives in online communities (e.g., on a course or workshop).

(4) Self-motivated participation: to attract a number of learners to join in a focus group or community because of a common learning interest.
(5) Share of learner-generated content: to allow learners to alter, develop, build and submit customised content and to encourage the sharing of learning materials generated by learners themselves, including personal profiles and various kinds of media-based content.
(6) Low-cost participation: no fee for registration and low-cost participation in SVWs.

Because of these innovative features, SVWs facilitate visual communication and social interaction to improve learners' motivation and engagement, delivering a student-centred active learning experience. SVWs have great potential to support learning activities in terms of the creation, distribution, and access of learning resources, collaboration and interaction, time and location independency, role changing (e.g., student and tutor) and achievement of learning outcomes. A growing number of universities and other educational institutions are exploring SVWs as a means to extend and enhance their existing VLEs.

The design of an augmented learning platform: a social learning approach for TEL

After investigating the impact of SVWs on the internet and identifying their innovative features, we believe that SVWs should be adopted in TEL, since they introduce socio-technical innovations on improving efficiency and cost effectiveness for learning practices, regarding individuals and organisations, independent of time, place and pace. The field of TEL emphasises the support of any learning activities through technology. As indicated by Wikipedia (2009), the well-known free encyclopaedia built collaboratively using a wiki, a learning activity can be described in terms of the:

(1) learning resources: creation, access, distribution and consumption of digital content; tools and services;
(2) learning objectives: to support learners in achieving their learning goals, respecting individuals as well as organisational learning preferences;
(3) learning actions: communication, collaboration, interaction with software tools;
(4) learning roles: a learning activity is carried out by various actors in changing roles (e.g., student, tutor, facilitator or education manager); and
(5) learning context: time and location.

Learning activities can follow different pedagogical approaches. The main focus in TEL is on the interplay between these activities and respective technologies. SVWs have great potential for TEL by offering the technological innovations to the learner and their learning environment that can support the delivery of flexible, seamless and personalised learning activities to learners. SVWs as innovative learning platforms enable learning activities to take place via social interaction in which learning content can be co-generated by participants. Learners are encouraged to become dependent on each other's knowledge and experience to the point of leading and teaching others (Arreguin 2007). Learning in SVWs is predominantly driven by the needs of the individual. Ondrejka (2008) points out that there is no explicit pre-set curriculum and that learning is regulated by the needs of the learners. Learning in SVWs primarily occurs through informal social practice, which mainly relies on self-motivation and self-management (Marsick and Watkins 2001). Therefore, there are some challenges in incorporating SVWs into formal learning in higher education (HE), which requires explicit curriculum design, indicative content development, learning materials management, learning outcomes achievement and accreditation (Lockyer and Patterson 2008).

We outline here the design of an augmented social interactive learning approach for TEL that has the potential to overcome these problems by supporting both informal and formal learning practices required in higher education. The authors propose an augmented learning platform, which incorporates SVWs as new components in traditional distance learning and integrates them with on-site teaching and learning. Figure 1 illustrates the augmented platform, which is designed to use an SVW as a visualisation integration interface to present online educational activities, interfaced to a Learning Management System (LMS) such as *Blackboard* (Blackboard 2009) and other student support systems.

The augmented platform is intended to support learning in SVWs through both formal and informal practices including workshops, group discussions, e-mentoring/e-tutoring and social events. The LMS such as *Blackboard* is responsible for hosting courses on the internet as a supplement to traditional

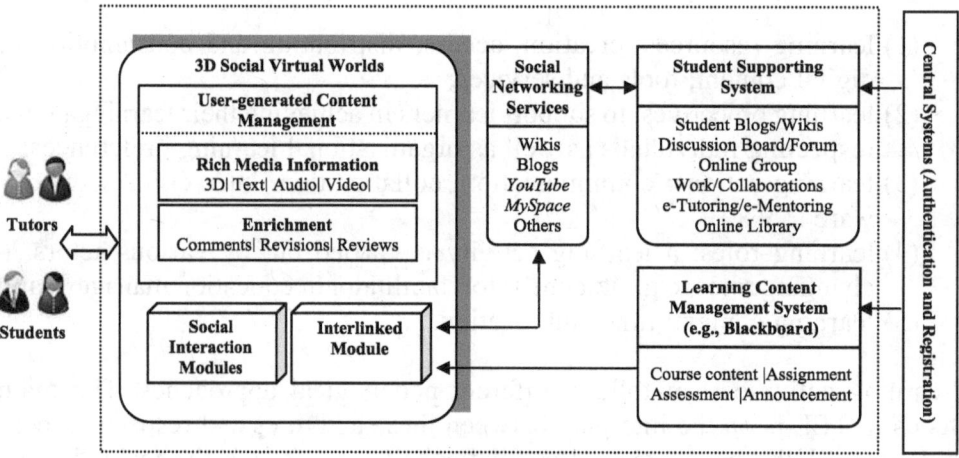

Figure 1. The design of an augmented social learning platform for TEL.

classroom courses. It is used for course management on this platform and allows tutors to upload and organise course materials including lecture notes, tutorial documents, reading lists, assignments, assessment and announcements similar to those used in classrooms and labs. Students can view and download these course materials and then complete and submit assignments to tutors for assessment via the LMS on the internet. The augmented learning platform relies on a customisable open architecture, authentication protocols and a scalable design that permits integration with other social networking services such as *YouTube*, blogs and *wikis* for student support systems. These social networking services are interlinked within an SVW such as *Second Life* to enhance the efficiency of communication between tutors and students and achieve real-time social interaction among them. As a result, learning on this augmented platform can be supported by exchange of knowledge, expertise and information through coupling with social networking services such as writing blogs, co-editing *wikis*, uploading videos on *YouTube*, joining *MySpace* and *Facebook* and sharing images on *Flickr*. Furthermore, an online library service can be linked into the system to enrich learning resources in the collaborative learning environment.

The augmented platform provides a social VLE, which allows students and tutors to download or upload learning content and conduct course-related discussions. It also provides a social online space that students would like to join in, where they not only work on course-related tasks, but also relax, socialise and talk with others. It enables students and tutors to connect and interact at both an academic level and a social level, in both formal and informal learning activities.

Discussions and experiments: prototyped social learning practices in SVWs

In order to validate the proposed augmented platform for TEL, some experiments are now described that involved actual learning practices prototyped in SVWs on this platform. At present, there are a number of SVWs existing that have great potential for integrating a 3D virtual world with other social networking services for education. In our research, we investigated the three most popular SVWs, namely *ActiveWorlds*, *Second Life* and *There*. Table 1 gives a comparison of the different features offered by these three SVWs.

It is clear from this comparison of the three most popular SVWs that *Second Life* offers distinguishing features in terms of multiple platform portability, powerful interactivity, rich media integration and professional service support. In addition, *Second Life* usage statistics highlight the tremendous growth rate in user engagement that *Second Life* maintained throughout 2008. *Second Life* users logged nearly 400 million hours in 2008, growing 61% over 2007 and users spend an average of about 100 minutes in-world per visit. This average session time is significantly greater than those seen with other popular

Table 1. Comparison of the most popular social virtual worlds.

SVWs Features	Active Worlds	Second Life	There
Visual representation	3D graphics but no real physics supported	3D graphics with full-featured physics supported	3D graphics with full-featured physics supported
Multiple platform support	Only for *Windows*	*Windows*, *Mac* and *Linux*	Only for *Windows*
Real-time interactivity	Basic scripting for simple manipulation	Full-featured scripting for complex interactive manipulation	No in-world scripting
User-generation content	Limited content can be uploaded only by virtual world owners	Most forms of content can be uploaded by any users and complex objects creation supported	Most forms of content can be uploaded by any users but no support for complex scripted items
Digital media integration	Streaming media supported for video and audio	Rich media supported for video, audio, animation and game.	Streaming media supported for video and audio
Service support	Few forms of support (e.g., FAQ and documentation)	Professional service support including instant messaging, live chat and a well-organised knowledge base	Mainly through a knowledge base

social networking services and reveals the uniquely high level of engagement users have with *Second Life* (Linden 2009). Based on the comparative analysis and evaluation, we selected *Second Life* as an SVW service to be integrated into the prototype augmented social learning platform in our project. A virtual campus was constructed in *Second Life* representing the real site of University of Westminster in the UK as shown in Figure 2a. As a visual interface of the augmented platform, it allows users to access a TEL environment where learning practices occur including workshops, seminars, invited speeches, group discussions and tutorial demonstrations. The virtual campus provides rich 3D representations of learning scenarios and uses hypermedia to improve delivery of learning materials beyond text. It has the capability of interlinking with an LMS such as *Blackboard* in conventional e-learning systems and integrating with other social networking tools such as *YouTube*, blogs and wikis. For example, a video tutorial demo can be played on a virtual computer monitor screen in *Second Life* and related supplementary videos can be hyperlinked and played in *YouTube*. The methods followed to deliver lectures in an SVW are very similar to those followed in the real world like *PowerPoint* presentations, video tutorials and guest lectures. But at the same time, it provides facilities that are only possible in an SVW. Since educational activities are diverse, the following learning practices have been chosen for further exploration in the SVWs on the augmented social learning platform.

E-tutoring/e-mentoring and career advice systems with social interaction

The impact of SVWs can have significant implications for the field of mentoring and tutoring. This is because, as previous research has pointed out, successful mentoring involves frequent and regular interaction but all sorts of barriers – such as time, work responsibilities, geographical distance and lack of trust – often reduce if not halt interaction (Bierema and Merriam 2002). TEL requires improving e-tutoring and e-mentoring systems through technological innovations, which tend to combine virtual learning components with some forms of human intervention. In the case of distance learning when students are geographically dispersed, it is usually impossible for mentors and mentees to meet face-to-face regularly. An SVW on the augmented learning platform is used to teleport students to the virtual campus of University of Westminster. An e-tutoring system has been prototyped and developed on the augmented learning platform as shown in Figure 2b. This gives the potential for students to discuss their work with their online tutors or mentors through their 3D avatars by real-time communication in the form of voice chatting, IM and even non-verbal expressive gesture and posture. Similarly, a virtual career office is set up in the virtual campus to provide e-mentoring for the development of students' career management and employability skills. With the utilisation of an SVW, an e-tutoring/e-mentoring system offers economical solutions, which impinge less upon the participants' time and effort, so that more frequent social interaction is easier to achieve and manage. E-tutoring or e-mentoring merges the traditional face-to-face mentoring relationship with

Figure 2. (a) The virtual campus of University of Westminster, UK; (b) An e-tutoring system prototyped in *Second Life* (Linden Research, Inc., San Francisco, CA, USA).

the emerging SVWs, and it is expected that this will be used increasingly as a social learning practice for TEL. It has several advantages, including open correspondence, access to more geographically isolated regions and efficiency of communication. As a result, students feel the e-tutoring/e-mentoring systems in the SVW are more attractive and engaging, enabling more meaningful discussions with the aid of visual communication and real-time interaction. Furthermore, multimodal social interaction in SVWs makes it easier for students to communicate with tutors and mentors thoughtfully and deliberately.

Social events for student-centred active learning

In universities, many academic social events are organised regularly by educators in order to enhance the students' active learning experience. The 'Degree show' is one example of a formal social event that aims to present students' exhibits and achievements to wider audiences. At the University of Westminster, the degree show for the M.Sc. computer animation course is organised annually in an on-campus gallery. It is regarded as important enough to be included as part of the students' final project assessment. Students are required to exhibit their work including concept art, storyboards, posters and animation production in the gallery. This is both a formal academic event and a social event, which aims to provide students with opportunities to interact with a wider audience, including potential employers from industry. The outputs from such social events including comments, suggestions and feedback can make a contribution to keeping the course curriculum up-to-date. However, the on-site degree show has significant limitations due to its high cost, limited time and restricted exhibition space.

In order to take advantage of the SVW for TEL, we launched the Computer Animation Degree Show 2008 in our virtual campus in *Second life* while the real on-site degree show was held in the on-campus gallery, the London Gallery West on 15–30 October 2008, as shown in Figure 3a. The feature of 'the learner as content producer' in an SVW allows students to put their visual works including poster design and animation video clips as user-generated content in the virtual gallery as shown in Figure 3b. Students can change and replace their exhibits whenever they want. Compared to the on-site degree show, the virtual exhibition in an SVW has great competitive advantages including low cost, removing the barriers such as limited time and space of exhibition, and being able to reach a much wider audience through the internet. Furthermore, the learner as content producer in this SVW has greatly spurred students' motivation, enhancing their creativity and productivity. More social events, such as university open days, can be prototyped on this augmented platform to reach wider audiences for course promotion. As a result, students are increasingly stimulated into active participation in social events in the SVW while achieving a student-centred active learning experience.

(a)  (b)

Figure 3. (a) The real on-site degree show held in London Gallery West; (b) The virtual degree show event organised in *Second Life* (Linden Research, Inc., San Francisco, CA, USA).

Role-playing simulation for the change of the roles

Role play is another important learning method used by educators, encouraging students to enact characters that will prepare them for the situations they might encounter in their work sectors. Role playing as simulation has been widely used as a part of many different teaching and learning activities. However, SVWs introduce a significant shift in TEL because learners are able to take on new roles and expand their identities in a virtual community as a supplement to a real-world identity. Also they have great impacts on the change of the roles of learners and instructors. Learners in SVWs develop their identity and knowledge both outside and inside the world by role playing. One such example would be the production of a clinic room in the virtual campus where the avatars participate in the role play of the interview between doctors and patients or salesman and customers.

There are many other learning practices such as workshops, seminars and conferences and even alumni reunions that can be prototyped and take place in the virtual campus. Based on the overall positive student feedback for these educational applications, the social advantages and student-centred learning experience offered by the augmented learning platform for TEL are seen to be strongly valued to students. Table 2 shows the performance evaluation of the augmented social interactive learning platform in comparison to traditional VLEs.

Conclusion

This article has presented a social learning approach that incorporates SVWs into conventional VLEs for TEL. By adding new dimensions for TEL that conventional virtual worlds cannot offer, it is seen that SVWs can be used to enhance various types of learning practices for TEL in terms of the creation, distribution, and access of learning resources, collaboration and interaction,

Table 2. The performance evaluation of the augmented learning platform in comparison to traditional VLEs.

	Traditional VLEs	The augmented social learning platform
Learning resources	• Primarily rely on content management system and focus on content retrieval and learning material download • Simple forms of content (e.g., text, image)	• Information/content enrichment oriented and supports user-generated content uploading and sharing • Integration of rich media-based content (e.g., animation, game, movie) for information visualisation
Learning actions	• Simple communication methods (e.g., emails, forums) • Less mechanisms for collaborative working • Basic and asynchronous interaction	• Multimodal communication (e.g., IM and live voice chatting, effective visual communication) • Effective team work and collaboration • Support of social interaction among users • Integration of other social networking services
Learning roles and context	• Fixed roles in learning activities (e.g., student, tutor, facilitator, or education manager) • Time and location independency	• Support of roles simulation including role changing and playing • Time and location independency while combining with some forms of human intervention
Learning experience	• Low level of engagement • Primarily passive learning experience • Limited self-motivation • Lack of mechanisms for creative thinking	• High level of engagement • Student-centred active learning experience • Stimulated self-motivation • Personalised and creative thinking encouragement

time and location independency, role changing (e.g., student and tutor) and achievement of learning outcomes. The augmented platform described above has been designed as an innovative collaborative learning environment where learning materials can be enriched with user-generated content through integration with rich media. Learning practices are supported by diverse social networking services over the internet such as *YouTube*, blogs and wikis. The platform uses an SVW as a visualisation integration interface to present online educational activities while interfacing with LMS and student support systems. The augmented learning platform has considerable advantages and strengths including improving student engagement and motivation, offering student-centred active learning experience and introducing socio-technical innovations. Preliminary experiments with the prototype augmented learning platform, including e-tutoring/e-mentoring and degree shows, have produced favourable responses from academics and students. In summary, SVWs are transforming the nature of learning as social practice in a collaborative environment. The augmented social learning platform will be able to support both formal and informal learning as well as facilitating social interaction, self-motivation, active engagement and creative thinking in TEL. More experimental educational activities are planned for the augmented learning platform in future work and these will be further evaluated through student feedback and progression analysis. It is intended to expand the platform by integrating more academic resources and services departments in HE such as career service, library service and training centres for TEL. However, social networking also raises challenging research issues about privacy, identity and intellectual property (IP) (Hendaoui, Limayem, and Tompson 2008). Furthermore higher level interaction (e.g., cognitive, motivational) has not yet been fully achieved in SVWs and researchers and practitioners are now attempting to address these complex natural multimodal interaction issues (Breslin and Decker 2007).

Acknowledgements
This project is partially supported by Education Initiative Centre and Online Learning Development Unit at University of Westminster, UK. Thanks to our M.Sc. computer animation students for the development of the virtual campus in *Second Life*.

References
Araujo, R.M., E.A. Rezende, T.S. Andrade, V.M. Chaves, M.G. Lopes, and B. Diirr. 2007. People in network, collaboration for action: New supporting requirements. Proceedings of 11th International Conference on Computer Supported Cooperative Work in Design, April 26–28, in Melbourne, Australia, 939–44.
Arreguin, C. 2007. *Reports from the field: Second Life community convention 2007 education track summary.* http://www.holymeatballs.org/pdfs/VirtualWorldsforLearningRoadmap_012008.pdf (accessed February 8, 2009).
Bierema, L., and S. Merriam. 2002. E-mentoring: Using computer mediated communication to enhance the mentoring process. *Innovative Higher Education* 26, no. 3: 211–27.
Blackboard. 2009. *Virtual learning environment.* http://www.blackboard.com/ (accessed September 2009).
Breslin, J., and S. Decker. 2007. The future of networks on the internet, the need for semantics. *IEEE Internet Computing* 11, no. 6: 86–90.
Churchill, E.F., and C.A. Halverson. 2005. Social networks and social networking. *IEEE Internet Computing* 9, no. 5: 14–19.
Cliburn, D.C., and J.L. Gross. 2009. Second Life as a medium for lecturing in college courses. Proceedings of the 42nd Hawaii International Conference on System Sciences, January 1–4, in Hawaii, 5–8.
Cunha, M., A. Raposo, and H. Fuks. 2008. Educational technology for collaborative virtual environments. Proceedings of 12th International Conference on Computer Supported Cooperative Work in Design, April 16–18, in Xian, China, 716–20.

Dell. 2009. *Dell island in Second Life.* http://www.dell.com/html/global/topics/sl/index.html (accessed February 2009).

Edinburgh. 2009. *The Virtual University of Edinburgh.* http://vue.ed.ac.uk/ (accessed February 1, 2009).

Garrett, J. 2009. *Ajax: A new approach to web applications.* http://www.adaptivepath.com/ideas/essays/archives/000385.php (accessed February 1, 2009).

Hendaoui, A., M. Limayem, and C.W. Tompson. 2008. 3D social virtual worlds, research issues and challenges. *IEEE Internet Computing* 12, no. 1: 88–92.

Hetherington, R., J. Bonar-Law, T. Fleet, and L. Parkinson. 2008. Learning in a multi-user virtual environment. Proceedings of IEEE 2008 International Conference on Visualization, October 19–24, in Columbus, OH, 99–105.

Kumar, S., J. Chhugani, C. Kim, D. Kim, A. Nguyen, and P. Dubey. 2008. Second Life and the new generation of virtual worlds. *IEEE Computer* 41, no. 9: 46–53.

Linden. 2009. *Second Life residents logged nearly 400 million hours in 2008 growing 61% over 2007.* https://blogs.secondlife.com/community/features/blog/2009/01/15/second-life-residents-logged-nearly-400-million-hours-in-2008-growing-61-over-2007 (accessed June 22, 2010).

Lockyer, L., and J. Patterson. 2008. Integrating social networking technologies in education: A case study of a formal learning environment. Proceedings of 8th IEEE International Conference on Advanced Learning Technologies, July 1–5, in Santander, Spain, 529–33.

Marsick, V.J., and K.E. Watkins. 2001. Informal and incidental learning. *New Directions for Adult and Continuing Education* 89: 25–34.

NASA. 2009. *CoLab virtual overview.* http://colab.arc.nasa.gov/virtual (accessed February 1, 2009).

NOAA. 2009. *NOAA virtual world.* http://slurl.com/secondlife/Meteora/177/161/27/ (accessed February 1, 2009).

Ondrejka, C. 2008. Education unleashed: Participatory culture, education, and innovation in Second Life. In *The ecology of games: Connecting youth, games, and learning*, ed. K. Salen, 229–52. Cambridge, MA: MIT Press.

Salomon, M. 2007. *Business in Second Life: An introduction.* Smart Internet Technology CRC, Swinburne University of Technology. http://www.smartinternet.com.au/ArticleDocuments/121/Business-in-Second-Life-May-2007.pdf (accessed February 1, 2009).

Weaver, A.C., and B.B. Morrison. 2008. Social networking. *IEEE Computer* 41, no. 2: 97–100.

Wikipedia. 2009. *Technology-enhanced learning.* http://en.wikipedia.org/wiki/Technology_Enhanced_Learning (accessed February 1, 2009).

How to enable knowledge exchange in *Second Life* in design education?

Aukje Thomassen[a] and Pete Rive[b]

[a]*Institute of Communication Design, College of Creative Arts, Massey University, Wellington, New Zealand;* [b]*School of Design, Victoria University Wellington, Wellington, New Zealand*

> The theory and lessons of knowledge exchange, in both a physical and virtual environment, suggest a framework for understanding the specific requirements for a digital design class in *Second Life*. Through teaching and observing students who were asked to complete a machinima project, our research provided examples of the strengths and the weaknesses of using *Second Life* for knowledge exchange. Learning is a process of creating knowledge, and so we observed the input and the output of the process. A literature review of knowledge creation considering the exchange of both tacit and explicit knowledge exchange informs our theory. Teaching occurred both remotely and, in person, in a media lab that included a physical presence of 33 students using networked computers and also allowed virtual presence in *Second Life*. The students also experienced a mixed-reality environment in which they collaborated sometimes in close physical proximity and sometimes only together in the virtual space. The exchange of tacit knowledge in a shared physical environment was regarded as a benchmark for knowledge exchange in *Second Life*, and we will conclude this article with some suggestions how that could be more closely simulated.

Introduction

Design faculties of universities across the world are faced with similar challenges that other organizations have faced due to the rise of creative industries and their creative class (Florida 2002). In the international arena, many research surveys have been conducted for an inventory and analysis of education within the creative industries. Several reports ('Design as a driver of user-centered innovation', 2009; 'Design, Arts and Communication', 2004; Friedman 1997; Thomassen and Bijk 2003) have shown that education still faces a knowledge gap between educational practice and professional practice. One of the reasons is that the educational market is no longer exclusive to universities. Over the years, private and public organizations dealing with education have extended their services in the realm of education quite successfully, such as Current TV, Mediamatics, and other businesses such as consultancy firms. On top of these challenges, the life cycle of products has decreased, and this is especially true in the field of digital media knowledge that can become outdated rapidly. Educational institutes are expected to keep up with this life cycle of knowledge. In order to meet these challenges, a knowledge vision has to be to be instilled (Thomassen and Bijk 2003; Von Krogh, Nonaka, and Ichijo 2000). Institutions of art and design education are, by nature, organizations that value learning and creativity. Education and knowledge creation are the core business of these organizations. As such, it is quite remarkable how poorly developed the notion of knowledge management is at an institutional level. Although, lecturers and educational staff put a lot of energy into enabling knowledge creation and facilitating learning at a student level, very few organizations have developed a knowledge vision of how they can enable knowledge creation at an institutional level (Thomassen 2003).

This article will discuss the aspects of knowledge management at an institutional level, by re-engineering educational practices and the implementation of knowledge exchange tools such as *Second Life*. *Second Life* provides an excellent case study environment to research creative collaboration and knowledge exchange (Bainbridge 2007; Bell and Trueman 2008; Boellstorff 2008; Castronova 2003, 2004, 2005, 2007; Lessig 2006, 2008). The digital rights management engine built into *Second Life* makes it a rich environment for researching knowledge exchange. The case study presented here discusses observations and questionnaires, which have been made during a 200-level studio course (July–November 2007) at Victoria University of Wellington, where they learned the basics of *Second Life* and machinima production, by using the 3D *Second Life* engine to create movies. This case study was designed to support research into knowledge sharing and creative collaboration in *Second Life*. We will provide some examples of student responses to *Second Life* as a virtual environment for knowledge exchange. Von Krogh, Nonaka and Ichijo cite Wittgenstein (1958), when they write, 'Knowledge is often in the eye of the beholder, and you give meaning to the concept through the way you use it' (2000, 6). This inherently subjective point of view takes us beyond the easily codified, explicit knowledge into the realm of tacit or hidden knowledge that is largely dependent on emotions, feelings, and the rich stimulation of the senses (Von Krogh, Nonaka, and Ichijo 2000). The theoretical framework for understanding knowledge exchange is provided by the work of Hedlund and Nonaka (1993) and Von Krogh, Nonaka and Ichijo (2000) who are well recognized in the field of knowledge management (Firestone and McElroy 2003; Hussi 2003). Many writers on the subject of tacit knowledge exchange have stated that this is possible only through face-to-face meetings, prolonged conversations, and good relationships (Dixon 2000; Teece 2000;

Von Krogh, Nonaka, and Ichijo 2000). However, it is possible to reframe the discussion around what enables tacit knowledge exchange and to consider the *Second Life* experience along a communication continuum. This article argues that rather than seeing tacit exchange as possible only through a face-to-face meeting, we can consider how closely a virtual face-to-face meeting can simulate a physical experience and explore the context and richness of the knowledge that can be exchanged (Rive et al. 2008).

The article will first discuss the foundation of knowledge and its relation with learning, followed by how it is enabled, all framed within the conceptual research of both Hedlund and Nonaka (1993) and Von Krogh, Nonaka and Ichijo (2000). The foundations and the framework will provide the lens to create an understanding of the presented case study of design education in *Second Life*. The conclusion will provide strategies and consideration when constructing an educational context within *Second Life* that has the potential to create knowledge.

Knowledge

In writing about knowledge, there is a clear need to describe how knowledge is perceived at an educational level. Knowledge is considered as information which is part of a meaningful and social context like a group or a virtual community (Boellstorff 2008; Weggeman 1997). As such, knowledge cannot exist outside an individual or a group (Boellstorff 2008; Maturana and Varela 1992). As a consequence of this approach, only information and not knowledge itself can be stored or transferred between individuals (Firestone and McElroy 2003; Von Krogh, Nonaka, and Ichijo 2000).

The only way knowledge can be exchanged is when knowledge is articulated into meaningful information. Articulation can be interpreted more broadly than just the codification of meaning into texts. Codification of meaning can occur by means of oral (speech, sounds, music), visual (body-movement, graphics), or even tactile codification. *Second Life* has the potential to support this concept of knowledge flow.

As a component of PhD research, this case study was set up to test the pedagogical approach to the articulation of knowledge, and also how technical solutions facilitate the flow of information. The model below illustrates how the research in the PhD case study has been organized around the distinctions between knowledge, information, and data.

The PhD research is targeted at the flow of knowledge throughout the different participants in the knowledge creation cycle throughout *Second Life*.

Enabling knowledge creation

'Learning is a process of creating knowledge' (Weick 1991, 119). This definition of learning perceives knowledge as both the input and the output of a

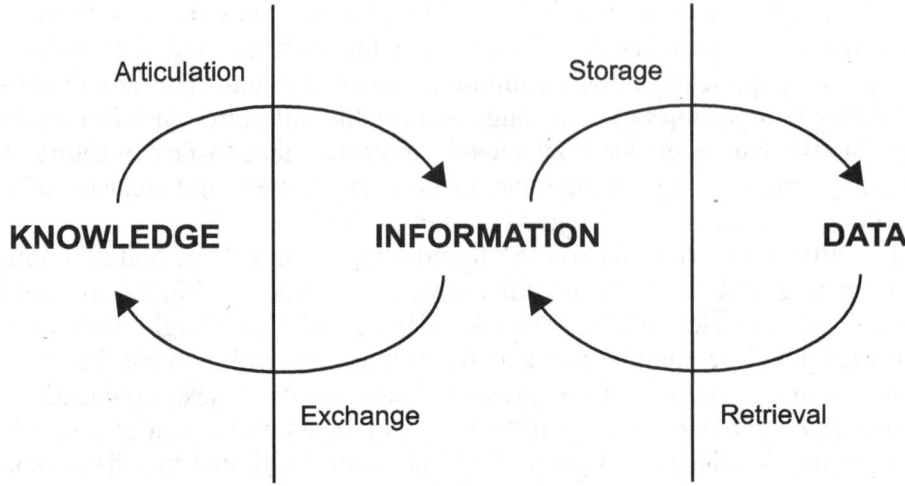

Figure 1. Data-flow model (Thomassen 2003).

learning process. This cyclic and behaviorist approach to learning is constructed into three interlocking stages: (1) collection of information, (2) processing and synthesizing, and (3) creation and evaluation (Renger 2000).

The data-flow model shows that collection of information is the first stage of this process (Figure 1). Information is collected by the participating students and can range from ideas, prior research outputs, investigations, or individual outcomes of prior learning cycles. All the information is collected to move toward the next stage. Processing and synthesizing focuses on information ordering, structuring, and synthesizing all with the purpose of moving to the third and last stage. Creation and evaluation is the final stage of this cycle. In this stage, the results will be evaluated. By evaluating the newly created knowledge, the cycle can be re-entered to create solutions for new problems or refinements on existing knowledge.

So, if agreed that learning is knowledge creation and that knowledge is the crucial vehicle for innovation and growth (Stewart 2001; Teece 2000) that must, in turn, meet the demands of the creative industries, then as a consequence this article will need to examine carefully what precedes knowledge creation, or in other words, what enables knowledge creation. Von Krogh, Nonaka and Ichijo (2000) argue for the following as the enablers of knowledge creation: (1) instilling a knowledge vision, (2) managing a conversation, (3) mobilizing knowledge activists, (4) creating the right context, and (5) globalizing local knowledge. For the purpose of this article, we will examine these key enablers briefly.

Instilling a knowledge vision

A knowledge vision needs to be instilled in order to start enabling knowledge creation as such. In the context of this article, the underlying knowledge creation process is design, in general. This vision embodies two types of knowledge: (1) strategic knowledge, and (2) operational knowledge. Strategic knowledge goals define the organizational core capabilities and describe the future knowledge needs of the organization. Operational knowledge goals make sure that normative and strategic knowledge goals will be translated into action (Abou-Zeid 2002; Probst, Raub, and Romhardt 2000).

Managing conversation

'It is quite ironic that while executives and knowledge officers persist in focusing on expensive quantifiable databases and measurement tools one of the best means for sharing and creating knowledge already exist within their companies ... conversations' (Von Krogh, Nonaka, and Ichijo 2000, 88). According to these authors, good conversations are the cradle of social knowledge and the most important enabler of knowledge creation. Educational facilitators in student-centered education are prone to valuing the beneficial effects of conversation on knowledge creation processes. In coaching student groups, educational facilitators often rely on conversations for the purpose of stimulating intellectual effort, promoting the articulating of progress, and structuring the workflow. These Socratic dialogs stimulate students to articulate on the knowledge and learning experiences acquired and promote critical reflection (Thomassen 2003).

Mobilizing knowledge activists

Knowledge creation can survive only when the participants are actively engaged. Knowledge management requires constructs that can be supported and embraced by the active participants in the knowledge creation construct. These activities are performed by the 'knowledge activist', which could be an individual, group, or function (Abou-Zeid 2002).

Creating the right context

Effective knowledge creation depends on an enabling context, which can foster ideas and facilitate the articulation, creation, and evaluation of experiences and knowledge. As such, the 'whole process of knowledge creation requires the necessary context or knowledge space' (Von Krogh, Nonaka, and Ichijo 2000, 7). Knowledge creation can happen only through an organizational structure that reinforces enabling and is aligned with strategy (Firestone and McElroy 2003; Hussi 2003; Thomassen 2003). However, this is more complex than just providing a knowledge space for co-operative learning to take place, students need to share a mutual frame of reference and structure, which, in this case study, is *Second Life* and a machinima course. The knowledge space was both virtual and physical; the virtual environment was the dedicated *MediaZone* island, in *Second Life*, which included zones for each project and offices for teachers, and the physical environment included a physical media lab with a large array of design workstations and projection screens.

Globalizing local knowledge

The knowledge derived from experience, however, is highly fit for exchange because it is not necessarily directly related to the specific contents of curricula, while keeping its relevance for students in the same discipline, and even across disciplines. As stated in the paragraph about the nature of knowledge, knowledge itself cannot be transferred as such. Articulation of knowledge into meaningful information, however, can be stored and manipulated by means of technology.

The knowledge vision case study

The case study for this research was conducted at School of Design of Victoria University in 2007. Students in the second year of the Digital Media Program of the Machinima Course used *Second Life* as a vehicle for knowledge creation and exchange.

Case study description – course outline

Initially, (using *Second Life*), the students were provided with several lectures on some of the theoretical and philosophical debates surrounding the *Second Life* ecosystem and how it can inform design knowledge vision supported by creative collaborations. The students had little previous exposure to the complexities of copyright, digital rights management, open source, Creative Commons, and the free software movement. The series of lectures set the context for the knowledge vision that outlined the debate surrounding digital identity, intellectual property ownership, and the non-rivalrous nature of digital assets. Also discussed were the benefits of creative collaboration and knowledge exchange in the *Second Life* ecosystem, according to several publications (Abramson 2005; Benkler 2005; Clippinger and Bollier 2005; Dibbell 2006a, 2006b; Ghosh 2005a, 2005b; Goldman and Gabriel 2005; Koster 2006; Lessig 2001, 2004, 2006, 2008; Ondrejka 2006; Raymond 1999; Suler 2006).

Also, the students were informed about the issues, as described by Lessig (2008), surrounding the tension between a commercial economy, concerned with buying and selling digital assets, and the almost zero cost of replication of digital resources that encourages a sharing economy (see, e.g., the Creative Commons movement). This tension was explained within the context of the *Second Life* economy and the digital rights management built into the *Second*

Life engine. The arguments of Richard Stallman Lessig (2001, 2004, 2006) and the Creative Commons movement were outlined to explain the spectrum of rights and the implications of creator ownership for knowledge exchange and creative collaboration.

Case study description – student participation

The case study was designed around a 14-week machinima project that examined the ability of the students to collaborate, communicate, and successfully complete a challenging design project in *Second Life*. The process of knowledge exchange was observed throughout the projects and was recorded through the different methods students used to communicate, both within *Second Life* and where they felt it necessary to augment *Second Life*, with other communication channels, including face-to-face meetings.

The method of investigation

The goal of this case study was to investigate the usage of *Second Life* in design education to facilitate knowledge creation and to get an understanding of the students' appreciation of *Second Life* in this context. To support this objective, the following data-collection methods have been used:

- (participatory) observations; a record of direct observations of student behavior and interaction was kept;
- user survey; an 'in-world' survey was distributed that enquired about their experiences; we interviewed other participants who were on the periphery of the student projects;
- repertoire analysis; student blogs that recorded conversations, showed pictures, and detailed their impressions were reviewed and analyzed (Rive 2008); and
- group interviews; finally each team was interviewed as they presented their project.

Evaluation of case study

A summary of our findings breaks down into the five key enablers from Von Krogh, Nonaka and Ichijo (2000).

Instilling a knowledge vision

The overall observation with regard to the first enabler was that the knowledge vision provided a theoretical framework for the students to experience the 'knowledge space' of *Second Life* first hand and enabled their knowledge exchange.

However, the students responded that they felt uncomfortable collaborating with people in a virtual world. They thought it was different to working face-to-face in class. They also found it harder to share ideas in *Second Life* compared to a physical studio working with other people, which makes sense as their collaborators were among the groups with whom they worked with in the same physical space. Nevertheless, they welcomed the anonymity of *Second Life* and felt it helped them to be less nervous about sharing ideas. As a result, some felt more inclined to express ideas and focus on how to communicate them effectively. Despite students' reservations, we suggested that the course provided a knowledge vision to the students that supported them in sharing and exchange.

Managing conversations

In sum, the students found that conversations were the essential means of enabling knowledge creation, and technology should be seen in that light. *Second Life* required augmentation with other technologies and face-to-face meetings. The students had the choice whether to only meet together in *Second Life* or to additionally meet physically in the media lab. Overall, the student teams successfully shared information in order to complete their machinima projects together. However, as there was some course assessment, they had a clear motivation to succeed in their creative collaboration using effective knowledge exchange. Fifty-nine percent of the students reported the team worked well together and were able to share ideas (using any means including face to face) and virtual objects in *Second Life*. The question of what is the motivation for knowledge exchange requires further investigation and research.

The students used a variety of ways to communicate with each other 'in-world,' and outside of *Second Life*. In a survey response from one of the students conducted in *Second Life*, the following was asked:

> Are ideas easier or harder to share in *Second Life* compared to a physical studio working with other people?

One reply illustrates the challenges faced:

> Yes, we tried do it all in *Second Life* and even brought headsets to talk over *Second Life* with but they didn't work. So in the end we moved closer to each other. I would guess that if the headsets worked it would have been better. [*sic*]

Managing the conversations in this case took place in real and virtual contexts, which the students did not mind. However, for a proper investigation of this second enabler, further work needs to be done around virtual conversations.

Mobilizing knowledge activists

In this particular case, the students felt that they acted as 'knowledge activists,' as did their educational facilitators, promoting their projects and creative collaboration. They valued this particular means of collaborations, as illustrated by their responses to: 'How would you value working in *Second Life*?'

> We made all our objects editable by each other, and so it was fun working with each other's designs. One person made an object, then another improved it, then another had their hand at making it look better, until the final product was a really impressive. *Second life* has the advantage of you actually being able to build an object that demonstrates what you're trying to get across, and this helps, but it seems to be a human reaction to prefer to discuss ideas face to face, so you can read what the person is [*sic*].

One team expressed how despite finding communicating harder in *Second Life* the 3D graphics helped to communicate their intentions:

> It's a little bit harder, but not too much of a barrier at all, especially in second life which is a very visual world so its easy to produce a mock up of an idea using blocks for example [*sic*].

When asked whether *Second Life* supported the free flow of knowledge creation, the students responded that they felt it was easier to share ideas:

> I can unlimitedly express my idea without thinking about what response I would get if I say so.

Students in this case were easily mobilized as knowledge activists as it was fully integrated in their course and it required the students to be actively engaged.

Creating the right context

The context in this case, the course, provided the virtual and physical knowledge spaces that were very effective knowledge enablers; however, it was a combination of both that provided the most effective means of knowledge exchange.

The class experienced technical difficulties with using voice chat in *Second Life* due to the school's network, so a majority was limited to text chat only. This contributed to a 60% response from the 33 student participants that ideas are harder to share in *Second Life* compared with working in a physical studio environment. It must also be noted that almost all the students were novice *Second Life* users, and that they had to learn how to use *Second Life*, as well as produce machinima, which is another demanding and complex enterprise. Initially, the class was given public domain software in *Second Life* in order to control their virtual camera. Eventually, a proprietary virtual camera system was bought, as it was easier to use. This was also the incentive for the students to partake in our survey, and they were only given the Linden dollars to buy the camera when everyone in their team had answered the question. Most teams felt the need to augment *Second Life* text chat with the class blog, email, and face-to-face meetings to improve communications.

When asked how they experienced the limitations of having limited facial expressions in *Second Life*, they responded that:

> The ability to express your ideas to people is quite restricted in *Second Life* because of the inability to show physical gestures and expression. Although you don't feel as much pressure to express yourself because you don't have the others glaring at you [*sic*].

As supported by Von Krogh and colleagues' research, creating the right context is of pivotal importance for a lively exchange of knowledge. In this case, the course offered a well-demarcated context, which also enabled the students to exchange beyond the course.

Globalizing local knowledge

This course helped the students to share their local work in a global context. *Second Life* was seen as an effective means of globalizing local knowledge as students shared a common virtual knowledge space with other *Second Life* participants. It would seem from their response that if the students had been able to use the 'in-world' voice communications, they would have found the experience easier, and a better simulation of working together face-to-face as this increases the immersion level of the world. But the students were flexible and even expressed that:

> Despite finding communicating harder in *Second Life*, the 3D graphics helped to communicate our intentions. It's a little bit harder, but not too much of a barrier at all, especially in second life which is a very visual world so its easy to produce a mock up of an idea using blocks for example [*sic*].

> I think it is working brilliantly, we are all contributing our own skills and learning from one another whilst still fulfilling [*sic*] our roles in the production. A very successful method of learning and effective work! [*sic*].

The students clearly opted for a global approach and moved beyond the assigned island in *Second Life*. They received feedback from the *Second Life* community and perceived that it added value in relation to collaborating and knowledge exchange.

Discussion

Machinima is similar to traditional film-making as it requires a team of people to collaborate. The case study investigated how to enable knowledge exchange in *Second Life* and identified the strengths and the weaknesses of the medium and the virtual environment. Von Krogh, Nonaka and Ichijo's framework (2000) provided knowledge creation enablers, which supported the analysis of knowledge creation performances in the *Second Life* context, and the clues for investigating the appreciation of *Second Life* by the students and also their perceived inadequacies. Within design education, learning is knowledge creation, and so from a pedagogical perspective, the effectiveness of *Second Life* as a learning experience can also be assessed in terms of knowledge creation.

It was found that *Second Life* approached effective simulated face-to-face meetings, deemed necessary for tacit knowledge exchange, but required augmentation with actual meetings, email, blogs, and voice communications. The subtleties of non-verbal communication expressed by complex facial expressions are missing from *Second Life* at present and are a large component of tacit knowledge exchange (Johnson 2006; Rive 2008). The findings were also supported by the literature from the disciplines of psychology, knowledge management, economics, and the study of presence in virtual reality (Rive et al. 2008). However, as stated by McLuhan (1994), 'the medium is the message' and virtual worlds such as *Second Life* provide a unique ecosystem that enables unique real-time knowledge exchange using 3D graphical tools (Davies 2003). *Second Life* is a highly creative and collaborative environment, with levels of participation far in excess of many other virtual worlds or massive multi-online role-playing games:

> Forty-two percent of Second Life users create objects from scratch using the built-in modeling system, and more than 44% have successfully sold an object to another user. Seventy-seven percent have bought one or more objects from other users, and 90 per cent have modified their avatar. (Ondrejka 2006, 11)

The *Second Life* digital rights management allowed for individual flexibility (if not complexity) for each and every avatar to choose whether to give a digital object away or to sell it. And for the students, each and every digital asset they created also became the embodiment of their knowledge, which was up for negotiation, while the students attempted to produce their machinima in *Second Life*. Knowledge creation and exchange were taking place on many levels within the student projects, within the student teams, between the teams, and between the digital objects and the receivers of those embodiments of knowledge.

Within *Second Life*, the name of the creator and the ancillary metadata is not attached to a person but to their avatar. Thus, the creations and the assets that were built up in *Second Life* contributed to the status and reputation of that avatar, and so the protection and security of those intangible assets became important to anyone who regularly participating 'in-world' and this also applied to virtual face-to-face meetings (Koster 2006).

A distinct and powerful feature of *Second Life* is the ability of the server and client to render 3D objects in real-time and to simultaneously enable interactivity with virtual objects. This has been missing from previous virtual environments that required expensive workstations and expert programmers to build objects, which once built were difficult to change (Grau 2003). Now, in

Second Life, you simply point at the ground and click either 'create' or 'edit landscape.' Real-time creative collaboration amounts to non-verbal communication between avatars and is another channel for tacit knowledge transfer in which an experienced coach can 'show how' rather than 'say how,' a task is performed (Leonard and Swap 2004). *Second Life* provides a rich media environment that enables tacit knowledge exchange directly related to the 3D medium.

Conclusion

An important focus of this research was exploring *Second Life*'s ability to facilitate and enable knowledge creation. This is where concepts and ideas from the field of knowledge management appeared to be highly applicable to an educational setting. An important requirement for this to successfully take place was for the knowledge creation enablers to be in place. The case study has shown how these can be implemented, although in order to improve presence in *Second Life*, it is believed that the platform requires the ability to transmit facial expressions from the user to their avatar, and thereby communicate greater subtlety in emotional states between avatars (Rive et al. 2008). Haptic interfaces for *Second Life* would greatly enhance the physical presence 'in-world' and non-verbal communications translating movement from the actual world to the virtual world. This aligns with one of the enablers as discussed in relation to 'Managing Conversations' in order to create knowledge we need to manage conversations. The participants of the case study felt that the current avatars have limited ability to interact on a physical basis and the gestures and animations are generated by preprogrammed scripts that do not extend far enough to create the 'perceptual illusion of non-mediation.'

Ultimately, the more *Second Life* can approach the fidelity of both physical and vocal communications, the closer it will come to an actual face-to-face meeting, and the more effective it will be at tacit knowledge creation (Riva and Ijsselsteijn 2003). This is reiterated in the introduction in which the notion of the bottlenecks of the creative industries was made, for example the current gap between educational practice and professional practice. *Second Life* has the ability to play a crucial role in narrowing this articulated gap provided that educators and others follow the knowledge creation and enabling philosophies laid out here. Workflow analysis is necessary to ensure that the right context is created to foster the desired knowledge vision. Both in and outside *Second Life*, conversations should be managed between the knowledge activists such that they feed into knowledge creation and exchange. While a tension between the principles of free software and digital assets for sale was observed, further research is required to investigate to what extent market mechanisms motivate knowledge exchange and to what extent they limit that exchange. This is an important question that goes to the heart of copyright and patent law, and is often debated with regard to software, and by implication digital design all within the context of the creative industries.

References

Abou-Zeid, E.-S. 2002. A knowledge management reference model. *Knowledge Management* 6, no. 5: 486–99.

Abramson, B. 2005. *Digital phoenix: Why the information economy collapsed and how it will rise again.* Cambridge, MA: MIT Press.

Bainbridge, W.S. 2007. The scientific research potential of virtual worlds. *Science* 317, no. 5837: 472–6.

Bell, L., and R.B. Trueman. 2008. *Virtual worlds, real libraries: Librarians and educators in Second Life and other multi-user virtual environments.* Medford, NJ: Information Today.

Benkler, Y. 2005. Coase's Penguin, or, Linux and the Nature of the Firm. In *CODE: Collaborative ownership and the digital economy*, ed. R.A. Ghosh, 169–206. Cambridge, MA/London: MIT Press.

Boellstorff, T. 2008. *Coming of age in second life: An anthropologist explores the virtually human.* Princeton, NJ: Princeton University Press.

Castronova, E. 2003. *Theory of the Avatar.* Online Social Sciences Research Network (SSRN).

Castronova, E. 2004. Right to play. *New York Law School Law Review* 49, no. 1: 185–210.

Castronova, E. 2005. *Synthetic worlds: The business and culture of online games.* Chicago: University of Chicago Press.

Castronova, E. 2007. *Exodus to the virtual world: How online fun is changing reality.* New York: Palgrave Macmillan.

Clippinger, J., and D. Bollier. 2005. A Renaissance in the Commons: How the new sciences and the Internet are framing a new global identity and order. In *CODE: Collaborative ownership and the digital economy*, ed. R.A. Ghosh, 259–86. Cambridge, MA: MIT Press.

Davies, R. 2003. *Virtual reality hardware and software: Complex usable devices? Communications through virtual technology: Identity community and technology in the Internet age.* http://www.emergingcommunication.com/volume5.html.

Dibbell, J. 2006a. Owned!: Intellectual property in the age of eBayers, gold farmers, and other enemies of the virtual state. In *The state of play: Law, games, and virtual worlds*, ed. J.M. Balkin and B.S. Noveck, 37–144. New York: New York University Press.

Dibbell, J. 2006b. *Play money: Or, how I quit my day job and made millions trading virtual loot.* New York: Basic Books.

Dixon, N.M. 2000. *Common knowledge: How companies thrive by sharing what they know.* Boston/New York: Harvard Business School/McGraw-Hill.

Firestone, J.M., and M.W. McElroy. 2003. *Key issues in the new knowledge management.* Boston: Butterworth-Heinemann.

Florida, R.L. 2002. *The rise of the creative class: And how it's transforming work, leisure, community and everyday life.* New York: Basic Books.

Friedman, K. 1997. *Design science and design education: The challenge of complexity.* Helsinki: University of Art and Design, UIAH.

Ghosh, R.A. 2005a. Cooking-pot markets and balanced value flows. In *CODE: Collaborative ownership and the digital economy*, ed. R.A. Ghosh, 153–68. Cambridge, MA/London: MIT Press.

Ghosh, R.A., ed. 2005b. *CODE: Collaborative ownership and the digital economy.* Cambridge, MA/London: MIT Press.

Goldman, R., and R.P. Gabriel. 2005. *Innovation happens elsewhere: Open source as business strategy.* Amsterdam/Boston: Morgan Kaufmann.

Grau, O. 2003. *Virtual art: From illusion to immersion.* Cambridge, MA: MIT Press.

Hedlund, G., and I. Nonaka. 1993. Models of knowledge management in the west and Japan. In *Implementing strategic processes: Change, learning and co-operation*, ed. P. Lorange, B. Chakravarthy, J. Roos, and A. Van de Ven, 117–44. Oxford: Blackwell.

Hussi, T. 2003. Reconfiguring knowledge management: Combining intellectual capital, intangible assets and knowledge creation. *Journal of Knowledge Management* 8, no. 2: 36–52.

Johnson, D.R. 2006. The new virtual literacy: How the screen affects the law. In *The state of play: Law, games, and virtual worlds*, ed. J.M. Balkin and B.S. Noveck, 245–56. New York: New York University Press.

Koster, R. 2006. Declaring the rights of players. In *The state of play: Law, games, and virtual worlds*, ed. J.M. Balkin and B.S. Noveck, 55–67. New York: New York University Press.

Leonard, D., and W. Swap. 2004. Deep smarts. *Harvard Business Review.* Reprint #7731. Boston, MA: Harvard Business School Publishing.

Lessig, L. 2001. *The future of ideas: The fate of the commons in a connected world.* 1st ed. New York: Random House.

Lessig, L. 2004. *Free culture: How big media uses technology and the law to lock down culture and control creativity.* New York: Penguin Press.

Lessig, L. 2006. *Code: Version 2.0.* 2nd ed., chapters 1–5. New York: Basic Books.

Lessig, L. 2008. *Remix: Making art and commerce thrive in the hybrid economy.* New York: Penguin Press.

Maturana, H.R., and F.J. Varela. 1992. *The tree of knowledge: The biological roots of human understanding.* Rev. ed. Boston/New York: Shambhala.

McLuhan, M. 1994. *Understanding media: The extensions of man.* London: Routledge.

Ondrejka, C.R. 2006. Escaping the gilded cage: User created content and building the metaverse. In *The state of play: Law, games, and virtual worlds*, ed. J.M. Balkin and B.S. Noveck, 158–79. New York: New York University Press.

Probst, G., S. Raub, and K. Romhardt. 2000. *Managing knowledge: Building block for success.* New York: John Wiley.

Raymond, E.S. 1999. *The cathedral and the bazaar: Musings on Linux and open source by an accidental revolutionary.* 1st ed. Beijing/Cambridge, MA: O'Reilly.

Renger, W. 2000. Nearness in distributed learning environments for the digital academy. In *Making and unmaking*, ed. T. Putnam, R. Facey, and V. Swayles, 344–55. Portsmouth: Design History Society.

Riva, G., and W.A. Ijsselsteijn. 2003. Being there: The experience of presence in mediated environments. In *Being there: Concepts, effects and measurements of user presence in synthetic environments*, ed. G. Riva, F. Davide and W.A. Ijsselsteijn, 3–16. Amsterdam/Washington, DC/Tokyo: IOS Press/Ohmsha.

Rive, P.B. 2008. Knowledge transfer and marketing in second life. In *Handbook of research on virtual workplaces and the new nature of business practices*, ed. P. Zemliansky and K. St. Amant, 424–38. Hershey, PA: Information Science Reference.

Rive, P.B., A. Thomassen, M. Lyons, and M. Billinghurst. 2008. Face to face with the white rabbit: Sharing ideas in second life. Paper presented at the IEEE International Professional Communications Conference, July, in Montreal.

Stewart, T.A. 2001. *The wealth of knowledge: Intellectual capital and the twenty-first century organization.* 1st ed. New York: Currency.

Suler, J. 2006. *The psychology of avatars and graphical space*. http://www.enotalone.com/article/2460.html (accessed November 2, 2009).

Teece, D.J. 2000. *Managing intellectual capital: Organizational, strategic, and policy dimensions*. Oxford: Oxford University Press.

Thomassen, A. 2003. In control: Engendering a continuum of flow of a cyclic process within the context of potentially disruptive GUI interactions for web based applications. PhD diss., University of Portsmouth.

Thomassen, A., and E. Bijk. 2003. Knowledge management in design education. In *Proceedings of the Conference WWDU 2002 World Wide Work Berchtesgaden*, ed. H. Luczak, A.E. Çakir, and G. Çakir, 183–5. Berlin: ERGONOMIC Institut für Arbeits und Sozialforschung Forschungsgesellschaft.

Von Krogh, G., I. Nonaka, and K. Ichijo. 2000. *Enabling knowledge creation: How to unlock the mystery of tacit knowledge and release the power of innovation*. Oxford/New York: Oxford University Press.

Weggeman, M. 1997. *Kennismanagement, inrichting en besturing van kennisintensieve organisaties*. Schiedam: Scriptum.

Weick, K.E. 1991. The nontraditional quality of organizational learning. *Organization Science* 2, no. 1: 116–24.

'Elven Elder LVL59 LFP/RB. Please PM me': immersion, collaborative tasks and problem-solving in massively multiplayer online games

Iro Voulgari and Vassilis Komis

Department of Educational Sciences and Early Childhood Education, University of Patras, Rion, Greece

Although there is strong evidence that massively multiplayer online games (MMOGs) constitute environments of social interactions and effective learning, we currently lack the tools for investigating the effectiveness of the social networks emerging as well as the cognitive aspects and knowledge acquisition such environments involve. Within this context, we present a conceptual framework for the investigation of the collaborative problem-solving processes emerging in such environments and we apply it in the investigation of a number of MMOGs through interviews and virtual ethnography. Our findings suggest the balanced convergence of multiple factors, such as the mechanics of the game, the design of the tasks, the collaboration and competition affordances and the content of the game, for the constitution of an effective environment for collaborative learning.

Introduction

The somewhat obscure phrase 'Elven Elder LVL59 LFP/RB. Please PM me' is a phrase very commonly used in the massively multiplayer online game (MMOG) *Lineage II(R)* among players looking to group with other players in order to tackle a particularly difficult task or a task where group participation is essential. Through this short, coded phrase, the players declare their virtual character's classification, their level, their intention to group and their preferred channel of communication. MMOGs constitute virtual environments rich in social interactions: users communicate and interact through text, audio and their virtual characters with other players within and beyond the game environment, through fora and player-developed sites. These interactions constitute an integral part of the gaming experience, decisive for the attainment of the goals of the games. MMOGs present many similarities to social virtual worlds like *Second Life(R)* or *Active Worlds(R)*, such as the 3D space, the graphical representations, the flexibility of user navigation within the environment and the avatars as the virtual representations of the players. They are also referenced to as virtual worlds, as a research area. However, they also present certain structural differences such as the different levels of flexibility of the environment, the integrated goal-oriented activities or 'quests', the levelling-up process of the players and the predominant role of collaboration and competition. In this article, we will focus on these features of MMOGs in relation to their impact on the learning processes emerging.

Over the past few years, the social aspect of MMOGs has been the focus of research examining the communication practices and the social interactions emerging (Steinkuehler 2003, 2004b; Atkinson et al. 2004; Ducheneaut and Moore 2004b; Young 2004; Hämäläinen et al. 2006; Williams et al. 2006). Latest research also suggests their potential as environments of informal learning (Steinkuehler 2004a; Galarneau 2005; Young, Schrader, and Zheng 2006; Schrader and McCreery 2008). The social context of gaming and the interactions of players in such environments constitute crucial factors for the emergence of learning and the construction of knowledge. Theories of situated cognition argue that the social context is an integral part of the cognitive processes affecting the learning activities and outcomes and not merely an independent factor (Garrison, Anderson, and Archer 1999). Learning is situated within the framework of social participation (Lave and Wenger 1991). A community of inquiry, a community where the participants engage in constructive, active dialogue and inquiry in order to negotiate meaning and construct knowledge, is being considered essential for an educational experience, deep learning and the development of higher order thinking, including questioning, reasoning and problem-solving skills (Garrison, Anderson, and Archer 1999).

Problem-solving, as a 'goal-directed sequence of cognitive operations' (Anderson 1980, 257), is being situated at the core of learning, either through the acquisition of problem-solving skills (Jonassen 2000) or as a method for attaining specific learning objectives, through constructivist-based educational approaches, such as problem-based learning and inquiry-based learning. MMOGs seem to comply with principles of these educational approaches. Playing an MMOG mainly involves the participation in a wide range of problem-solving activities and tasks, either individually or collaboratively (Steinkuehler 2006). When the players start playing an MMOG, they are presented with the problem to be solved: the initial state, the goal they have to accomplish and the rules of the game. The players, though, have to solve a number of sub-problems and achieve a number of sub-goals during the game in order to achieve the general goal. The ill-defined problem (Mayer 1992) presented initially is separated into well-defined sub-problems. Furthermore, the open-ended and flexible structure of the narrative allows the users to additionally select their own tasks, actions and strategies and set their own goals (Juul 2007) such as gain more experience in a specific field, acquire more knowledge, explore the environment further, collect objects to be exchanged or traded.

The task-oriented and goal-oriented approach integrated in the MMOGs as well as their social nature formed the main motivation of our research. These concepts were used to frame an investigation of the potential of MMOGs, as compared to an effective learning environment, for the acquisition of knowledge as well as the development of higher order thinking skills such as collaborative problem-solving skills.

As a new field of investigation and as highly dynamic and social environments, MMOGs are 'immune to traditional tools' of analysis (Gee 2007, 83) and require the development of new tools and frameworks of research (Gee 2007, 86; Schrader and McCreery 2008; De Freitas 2009). Our research is situated within this context. We present a conceptual framework for the investigation of the collaborative interactions, and more specifically the collaborative problem-solving activities in MMOGs and apply this framework to the investigation of different MMOGs. In this article, we review literature in the area of cognition, learning, collaborative problem-solving and computer-mediated communication and relevant research in the area of MMOGs. We identify specific axes of investigation relevant to our focus, and we examine features of games and perceptions of gamers in relation to this framework.

Conceptual framework

The motivation of the players, the 'fun' of the game, is one of the strongest aspects of MMOGs. The immersion of the players, their passion and enthusiasm identifies with what is described as 'flow experience', at which state the users concentrate and are deeply involved in the activity (Csikszentmihalyi 1992; Prensky 2001; Stapleton and Taylor 2003; Kiili 2005). This involvement of the players is triggered not so much by the motivation to solve the global problem and attain the final goal, which in most of the cases is long-term, but rather by the gaming experience itself. Intrinsic motivation of the game factors in the development of online communities or affinity spaces, as described by Gee (2007, 75), revolve around the learning and mastering of the game. Beyond the motivation behind a problem-solving activity and as a prerequisite for the appeal and the effectiveness of a game lays the design of the unit of the player's activity: the task itself. The aim of the design within a learning environment is to produce tasks that are motivating for the players as well as cognitively intriguing and effective (Mayer 1998).

In an attempt to define the concept of the 'problem to be solved' in an MMOG, we refer to the two main playing styles encountered in most

MMOGs: player versus player (PvP) and player versus environment (PvE) (Myers 2007). PvE activities involve the interaction of the player with the environment. They constitute well- or semi-defined problems such as the quests each player has to accomplish in order to progress and evolve through the game. Through the quests the players build up their skills, acquire relevant knowledge and explore the mechanics of the game. PvE tasks can be accomplished either individually or collaboratively by a group of players. PvP activities involve competitive interaction among players requiring at least two players and ranging to contests among large groups of players. These mechanics involve a number of different, peripheral activities and tasks that will also help players progress. These latter activities can also be individual, such as the collection of items and the crafting of a new weapon or armour, or collaborative, such as the participation in the economic system of the game through, for example, trading with other characters, forming and managing a group, negotiating and reaching common agreements with other players.

The environment-related activities have a more or less standardised and repetitive format and a predefined strategy for solving them, and are actually often criticised by the players, as, for example, in the case where the players have to kill hundreds of computer-generated monsters in order to gain experience points (activity referred to by players as 'grinding'). The tasks involving interaction with other players, though, seem to be more open-ended, more flexible and dynamic, permit the employment of multiple approaches for their solution and, in most of the cases, require more sophisticated player strategies. Both type of tasks are interconnected and integrated into the narrative of the game. Although they are presented as sub-problems for solving the global problem of the game, even after a few hours of playing, it becomes apparent that the final goal, for example, the restoration of peace in a kingdom, can never be actually attained.

For setting the conceptual framework for the investigation of MMOGs, with respect to the cognitive and motivating aspects of the collaborative problem-solving processes emerging, we have identified two main axes that we will elaborate on in the next two sections: (1) task features: the structure, design and cognitive content of the problems or tasks, and (2) interaction features: the interactions, communication and collaboration affordances of the environment mechanisms. These two axes are partially consistent with the Community of Inquiry Model as proposed by Garrison, Anderson and Archer (1999). Garrison and colleagues proposed a model for the sustainment of an effective community for the development of critical thinking and knowledge acquisition, comprising three core elements: the cognitive presence, the social presence and the teaching presence. Although their model was mainly applied in text-based asynchronous environments, we hypothesise that an effectively designed task in an MMOG may scaffold cognitive presence of the players/learners, while appropriate affordances of the environment should be able to support their social presence. In MMOGs, there is no educator present to manage and assess learning processes and outcomes. Players are learning the game through their interaction with the system and with other players, forming what was described by Galarneau (2005) as 'spontaneous communities of learning'. We, therefore, assume and will try to investigate the fact that the role of the teacher is played by the environment itself and the interaction with peers, with the teaching presence integrated within the design of the tasks and the interaction affordances.

The MMOG quest as a problem-solving task for learning

The overview of research in the area of problem-solving in games such as chess by Frensch and Sternberg (1991) indicates that the key for the acquisition of expert knowledge and the development of high-level problem-solving skills is the meaningful encoding of information in memory and the integration of new knowledge into coherent schemata. Meaningfully encoded domain-specific information, integration of the new knowledge into coherent schemata, acquired skills and the metacognitive knowledge or metaskills to select and apply the appropriate knowledge and skills seem to be the key features of an expert problem-solver.

The issue arising at this point is the knowledge, the skills and the domain-specific information acquired by the player/learner, which are linked to the educational objectives (Mayer 1998; Young 2004). In short, what do we want the learner to learn through the activity? The acquisition and development of higher order thinking skills, such as skills for cooperation and collaborative problem-solving, could be one objective for the tasks in an educational setting or it could be enhanced with the acquisition of domain-specific knowledge such as history, physics or geography. Furthermore, system functions for the examination and assessment of the internal schemata formulated by the players/learners, at predefined intervals through the game play, could ensure the coherence and consistency of these internalised schemata and the validity of the integration of further knowledge and skills and prevent possible misconceptions from the part of the players/learners.

'Will' or motivational skills have also been described by Mayer (1998) as a critical 'prerequisite for successful problem-solving'. The individual interest, the situational interest emerging from the characteristics of the environment, the sense of self-efficacy and also the attribution of any success or failure to the effort invested rather than on the ability of the person seem to be the main sources of motivation for an effective problem-solving activity (Mayer 1998). The individual interest is related to the personal interest of the learners in the activity, while the situational interest is a feature of the environment and the tasks. The learner needs to be able to understand the purpose behind the solution of a problem, the meaning behind a task. The narrative of the game provides the context for the problem-solving activities (Kafai 1994). Integration of the tasks into a consistent narrative provides an authentic and realistic context of the purpose for the solution of each task and quest (Norton and Wiburg 2003). The sense of self-efficacy is related to the learners' perceptions of their abilities to solve the tasks. The immersion to the environment is reinforced by the sense of control over the task and the feeling that the task can be accomplished (Csikszentmihalyi 1992). The correspondence of the player's skills with the demands of the environment, the gradual progression of the character (Ducheneaut et al. 2006), the support throughout the game and especially for the new players, the easy and fast levelling at the beginning of the game for building up the confidence and skills of the new players constitute techniques incorporated into the games that seem to address this aspect. Academic performance is, finally, related to whether a learner attributes the success or failure to the effort invested in a task rather than to other external or internal factors (Mayer 1998). Such a feature sustains the engagement of the learner with a task and reinforces multiple attempts to solve the problem.

Transfer of the acquired knowledge and skills to similar problems is also crucial for the academic performance. Isomorphic spaces of tasks permit this transfer. As is the case in most MMOGs, the tasks are interdependent. The player has to have already accomplished specific earlier tasks, in order to progress to later ones. The solution of each problem not only works well for the problem but also works well as a component of later, more difficult problems (Gee 2004). This interdependence, the integration of the tasks 'into the larger context of the game' (Salen and Zimmerman 2005), provides a meaning to the game and seems to constitute an important factor for successful game playing as well as for the effective acquisition of knowledge (Hoppe and Ploetzner 1999; Gee 2003).

With respect to the representation of the problems, the visual and audio quality of the environment, the realism, the sound effects, the actions of the characters and the design of the interface do not only add to the emotional interest of the players but they may also play an integral part in the effectiveness of the tasks and the quality of the interactions of the player with other players and with the environment (Manninen and Kujanpää 2005). For example, as in the case where a player can hear the enemies approaching, even though s/he cannot see them yet or may get non-verbal audio cues for imminent danger and therefore can be better prepared and timely plan his/her reaction.

Drawing from the principles of situated cognition and ecological psychology, Young (2004) identified the duals of agent–environment, affordance–effectivity and perception–action as critical components within a learning scenario and an MMOG. These duals involve the reciprocal relationship between the features and the possibilities of the environment and the potential and actions of the users. The learning environment allows the learner to select their goals and try different approaches and strategies. Describing the features of good problem-solving situations, Greenberg (in Norton and Wiburg 2003) identified the complexity of the problem, so as to allow for multiple solving approaches. The learners are provided with the opportunity to test their hypotheses and select the most appropriate solution.

The interaction of the player with the environment defines the perception of the player for the game and the gaming experience. Meaningful play can emerge only when the relationship between the player actions and the system outcomes is 'discernible' (Salen and Zimmerman 2005), when the player is provided with immediate feedback and knows what happens when s/he takes an action.

Supporting task-oriented interactions

The design of the affordances, the rules and the functionality of the environment play a decisive role in the quality of effective collaborative interactions among players. The features for ensuring such interactions seem to be the promotion of productive interactions and cooperation rather than aggressive competition (Dillenbourg 1999), the availability of appropriate channels and mechanisms for the support of communication and collaboration in game and beyond the game and the discouragement of aggressive behaviour. In our previous work (Voulgari and Komis 2008), we reviewed the components and functionalities of the environment that could satisfy these features (summarised in Table 1). We employed Dillenbourg's (1999) definition of collaborative learning, where three broad areas of focus were identified: the learning processes and outcomes, the number of people involved and the different forms of interaction. We transferred these areas of focus to the design of online game environments within an educational context. We distinguished three main relevant axes: the structure and features of the problem-solving activities or quests, the size of the groups formed in game and the forms of interaction emerging.

Another issue a computer-mediated communication environment for learning has to address is the sense of interaction with other 'real' people or what is described by Garrison in his Community of Inquiry Model (Garrison, Anderson, and Archer 1999) as 'social presence'. Social presence contributes to the attainment of affective and cognitive goals. The emotional expression of the participants, the open communication and the cohesion of the group are indicators of the social presence and are directly influenced by factors such as familiarity, skills, motivation, organisational commitment, activities and length of time in using the medium (Garrison, Anderson, and Archer 1999).

Research methodology

Having set a framework for investigation, we applied the identified aspects of the game design relevant to the emergence of effective collaborative problem-solving activities for learning to the collection of data through immersive virtual ethnography (Hine 2000) in specific MMOGs; online and offline interviews; and study of game-related websites, documents and fora. More

Table 1. Summary of environment features for collaborative interactions in an MMOG.

Environment features	Components for satisfying the features
Collaboration is an essential prerequisite for succeeding in the game.	• Tasks with high risk penalties • Tasks cannot be completed without the participation of more than one character
Features for the facilitation of collaboration	• Visibility among the characters • Audibility of voice • Support of verbal as well as non-verbal communication • Physical proximity of the players
Establishment of links and affinity among players	• Encouragement of social chat • Real-life friends • Severe penalties
Distributed knowledge	• Knowledge integrated into tools • Different and complementary roles
Shared goals	• Common interests in clans/guilds and parties
Heterogeneity of resources	• Different and complementary roles
Support of verbal communication (discussions)	• Support of high-level questions, explanations and collaborative problem solving processes such a as aggregation, conflict creation, revision and solution
Support of non-verbal communication (actions)	• Realism of image • Affordances for player actions and reactions
Group formation for appropriate problems and players	• Group-matching functionalities
Support communities of practice formation	• Original documentation of the game is minimal. For discovering the game in-depth, user contribution is required

specifically, we created two virtual characters and engaged in the online game (massively multiplayer online role-playing game) *Lineage II(R)* for the course of 18 months (2006–2008), logging in and playing the game for approximately 14 hours per week, as well as the web-based, multiplayer real-time strategy game *Tribal Wars(R)* (Greek server version, World 1) for seven months (June–December 2008) for approximately one to two hours per week. We became members of in-game clans and tribes (structured groups of players) and immersed in the players' online and offline interactions, keeping field notes and collecting game screenshots, videos, logs and in-game forum content. Through this ethnographic study, we acquired deeper understanding of the practices within these environments as well as a qualitative background for our research framework (Ducheneaut et al. 2006). These two multiplayer games have an entirely different format and style in relation to the environment design and their content, with the intense collaboration of the players for achieving a common goal, as their common feature. We selected the particular games mainly due to their popularity as well as for cross-examining our findings with studies focusing on other multiplayer games (Nardi and Harris 2006; Steinkuehler and Williams 2006) such as the *World of Warcraft(R)* (*WoW*), a massively multiplayer online role-playing game (MMORPG) similar to *Lineage II(R)*, which now holds the primary share in the MMOG market (Meredith, Hussain, and Griffiths 2009; MMOData.net – http://mmodata.net/; Entertainment Software Association – http://www.theesa.com/facts/pdfs/ESA_EF_2009.pdf).

We conducted 15 semi-structured interviews of MMOGs players, one of them online and one focus group, within the course of six months (December 2008–May 2009) asking them about their motivation for playing games, their interactions with other players, their perceptions on the content and affordances of the environment and the impact they feel the game has on them. We publicised our call for participants through emails to students at the University of Athens and the University of Patras, through a dedicated *Facebook* group and a web page hosted at the site of the Department of Educational Sciences and Early Childhood Education at the University of Patras (Research Call; http://www.ecedu.upatras.gr/voulgari/) and also through our groups in *Lineage II* and *Tribal Wars*. Most of the participants who responded were male, with the exception of one female for the interviews and three female students who participated in the focus group. Most of them were expert gamers, except one novice male player, mainly living in urban areas (Athens and Patras), aged from 17 to 50 and from a variety of educational and professional backgrounds. The interviewees were players of different MMOGs. Namely, the games the interviewees mentioned playing were: *WoW(R)*,[1] *Lineage II(R)*,[2] *Left4Dead(R)*,[3] *Tribal Wars(R)*,[4] *The West(R)*,[5] *EVE Online(R)*,[6] *DotA(R)*[7] and *Age of Conan(R)*.[8] We decided to address a wider range of games, for testing the generalisation of our framework of investigation and for identifying emerging common patterns or issues through different types of MMOGs. Finally, we studied game-related sites and fora, both official as well as user-developed, specifically for the games mentioned during the interviews and for the games in which the virtual ethnography took place, for enhancing our perception of these games, for cross-referencing our findings and for collecting data relevant to our research.

Results

Based on the features of an effective collaborative problem-solving environment, as described in our framework, we investigated the relevant perceptions of players, supported by material collected through our ethnographic research and data from fora and websites as described in the research methodology section. It is not our intention to extrapolate on the design of all MMOGs or apply our conclusions to the general population of players, but rather try to shed some light on specific core elements of MMOGs and features that have the potential to support learning in a larger educational context. In this section, we will elaborate on the key issues that emerged during this research.

Defining the expert

Although in the investigation of problem-solving processes there is usually a reference to the expert problem-solver as the one with the most effective strategies for solving the problem, in the case of MMOGs, the criteria for defining the expert do not seem to be as clear. During their investigation of the social behaviour of experts in massively multiplayer online role-playing games, Huffaker et al. (2009) identified two dimensions of expertise: achievement and performance, with achievement referring to the level of the player and performance referring to how efficient the player is. Although efficiency is a strong indication of expertise, we were concerned about adopting the level of the virtual character as a per se indication of expertise. In MMOGs, it has been observed that players exchange game accounts helping each other to reach a higher level, buy high-level characters from other players or dedicated companies or hire companies to level up their characters even though such an activity is illegal and punishable (Yee 2006a; Dibbell 2007). Furthermore, as participants in our research commented, the level and the experience points gained by the player do not necessarily constitute a criterion of expertise, since, for example, the leader of a group may be focused more on supporting other members and levelling up the group than in levelling up his/her own character. We tried therefore to review the concept of the 'expert player' in an attempt to later identify the skills acquired or practised through an MMOG.

When the players in our research were asked about their perception of a 'good player', the answers varied. Interviewed players would consider a good player the one with the most extensive knowledge of the game, or the player with the best communication, collaboration or strategy planning skills. It is difficult to define the expert in an MMOG mainly due to the variety and wide range of tasks and roles available. Indicatively, some answers elicited during the interviews about the good player were 'the one who has explored the content', 'the one who acts efficiently with respect to his/her gear', 'the one with a good real-life personality', 'the one with the best behaviour towards other players', 'the one who reaches his/her objective more efficiently', 'the one that plays for the game and not for winning'. Features of the good player seem to combine, therefore, in-game skills with real-life personality traits.

Good players, in relation to their knowledge of the game, are rewarded with rare items, unlocking of new territories available only to high-level players, respect or fear from other players. In addition, good players, in relation to their behaviour and interaction with others, seem to gain respect from co-players and even more opportunities to cooperate with others, as also commented by our interviewees.

Learning in MMOGs

When investigating MMOGs from the perspective of the learning occurring, it is also essential to address the issue of the type of knowledge acquired through these games, the processes through which learning is acquired and whether it can be transferred to other domains. MMOGs have to be challenging enough for motivating the players but also not too complex and too difficult to learn and progress, to avoid discouraging new players. Beginners are supported by peers and by built-in features such as non-player characters (NPCs) or areas designated for beginners. Processes such as upgrading of skills, demands from the game and the complexity of character manipulation are incremental. From this point on, knowledge of the game is a matter of experience and practice as well as of the personal interest and the personality and skills of the player. The repeated format of the quests throughout the game directs the practice of specific skills which can be then applied to later quests. The progression of the designed tasks and quests ranges from tasks requiring simple strategies to more sophisticated ones, which, although relying on the prior acquisition of these simple strategies, require more factors to be considered and manipulated. This linear progression ensures that by the time the player has reached the higher levels of game play, s/he has already mastered the appropriate strategies and skills to cope with more demanding problems. Furthermore, the expert player has not only learnt the appropriate actions in the game but also understands the implications of these actions on the environment (Reeves, Brown, and Laurier 2009). With experience, the players acquire a broader perception of the game, progress and upgrade their resources. Our interviewees reported that failure in a task very rarely discouraged them. They reported that failure in a task would only make them assess the situation and their performance, find their weak points and try again. In some cases, they may attribute the difficulty of a task to the poor design of a game. As Reeves, Brown and Laurier (2009) also suggested in their research on the acquisition of expertise in the game *Counter Strike(R)*, players became experts through differentiating repetition, trying out different tactics, responses and tools.

Reference to resources and information external to the game, such as fora, websites, external applications and tools, official or user-created, is essential. All the interviewees commented that it is probably impossible to become a good player without referring to external resources. Some of these resources are also reviewed in Meredith, Hussain and Griffiths' (2009) scoping study of MMORPGs.

The perceptions of the players interviewed with respect to what they believe they are learning from the game were of particular interest. Although they reported that they do not feel they learn something they can use in real life and commented that they only learn how to play the game, a wide range of different skills practised emerged in the answers of the players, even of those who reported that they learn nothing. The interviewed players referred mainly to the practice of managerial or organisational skills:

I believe that a good guild leader could become a good manager. (*WoW* player)

Maybe I learnt a bit more about trading. How to buy cheap and sell with profit. (*Lineage II* player)

The players also reported that they learn more 'about human behaviour' or learn from the interaction with people of different cultures, experiences and backgrounds. They have to cooperate with others, follow a specific code of behaviour, assign and play roles, resolve conflicts, impose or accept the social consequences of their actions and negotiate. Some of the players also reported the underlying collaboration and teamwork required in all the MMOGs as an area of skills developed through play. This is probably an issue requiring further investigation: whether or not social skills, such as collaboration and communication, can be developed through an MMOG, whether they can be transferred beyond the game and under which conditions.

According to interviewees' comments, transferable skills or knowledge acquired by the game mainly concern the interaction of the player with the interface and the mechanics of the game, and only in the case that the games have a similar style, content or interface.

Motivation

Dickey (2007) discussed the design elements that promote intrinsic motivation for learning in MMORPGs in relation, mainly, to the character selection and the narrative of the game. She identified choice, control, collaboration, challenge and achievement as the main motivating features of MMORPGs referring to design mechanisms such as the quest selection, the progress of the player and the chat and communication tools. These features also came up in our respondents' answers. The issue of character selection and narrative will also be further discussed in later sections.

The majority of our respondents attributed the appeal of MMOGs to their social aspect. Previous research has also identified the social aspect of gaming and the interaction with other real people as one of the main motivators for the participation in an MMOG (Lazzaro 2004; Ducheneaut et al. 2006; Williams, Caplan, and Xiong 2007). Interaction with other people, from different parts of the world and with different backgrounds, also came up in our interviews as one of the main reasons players engage in an MMOG. The age, the interests, the behaviour of other players seem to be the factors influencing the selection or the rejection of a game. A 17-year-old *Lineage II(R)* player reported:

> It [the game] provides entertainment, mutual support in the clan, communication with other players, and meeting people above all [...]. Even though I like playing, I consider it a waste of time. But I still like playing.

One of our clan members in *Lineage II(R)* also commented during an in-game chat:

> Lineage is 50% xp [levelling up the character] and 50% socializing.

The sense of freedom emerged from our interviews as another motivating aspect for the game. It refers to the freedom of the player to navigate into the content, the freedom to select specific tasks, the freedom to select the mode and pace of playing. Through the variety of tasks available, each player may find the tasks closer to his/her preferences. The flexible structure of the narrative allows the players to select and focus their activities on specific tasks. A player, for example, not keen on fighting monsters, or not really interested in levelling up, may decide to spend more of his/her time on fishing, seeding or trading game items. This variety of tasks and activities available and the personalisation of the playing style ensure that a wide range of players may be interested and engaged in the game for longer.

Another motivational dimension of the game, and particularly for MMORPGs, seems to be the representation of the environment and mainly the graphics. Many of our respondents referred to the graphical representation of the environment and of the virtual characters as an important factor for the selection of a game. Sophisticated graphics, audio and animation seem to support the immersion of the player into the environment:

> When you start your character [...] you are in a forest. And this forest is so lively that you think you are in there. You listen to the birds, the rivers, the weather conditions, and this captivates you. (*WoW* player)

The players may personalise their avatars by selecting the facial expressions, the hair style and colour, the outfit of the character. The environment offers a large number of different areas to visit and explore, ranging from forests and lakes to cities, dungeons and remote galaxies. Audio cues facilitate the perception of the surrounding area and activity. Specific sounds, for example, indicate that an enemy is approaching and help the player react in time, or different styles of music denote a peaceful or threatening area.

Although game rewards were not explicitly mentioned as a motivating element of the game, most of our interviewees elaborated on the time they spent trying to collect items for manufacturing a new weapon, or on the sense of achievement they had when they could buy a new outfit or an item for their virtual character, or when they reached a higher level and were therefore able to access more of the content of the game environment. These rewards seemed to constitute factors that could keep a player in the game for longer, consistent with the findings of Ducheneaut et al. (2006) who identified rewards in the game as a strong motivation for players, increasing their play time.

Task design

As described in our conceptual framework, tasks may be either relevant to the interaction of the player or players with the environment (PvE) or with the interaction among players (e.g., PvP, group management, decision-making, collaboration), with PvE tasks being more closed, predefined and repetitive and player-interaction-related tasks being more open-ended, flexible and dynamic. Although PvE tasks or quests aim at familiarising the player with the environment, helping him/her progress and acquire resources such as in-game currency or items, some of our players admitted that they would rather avoid them and only engage with them when necessary, mainly because they considered them 'boring' and repetitive. On the other hand, player-to-player interactions or PvP seemed to attract the interest of most interviewees, consistent with Lazzaro's (2004) findings that the participation of other players increases the difficulty and variety of emotions experienced:

> […] but whether you will win or not, depends on the other player. And this is the part of the game which is amazing. (*EVE Online* player)

> It's different when you have to deal with another human being in online games. You don't know how the other person will react. (*Lineage II* player)

> […] you see a new player and s/he may eventually win the battle. S/he may set his/her ship up in a way that you don't expect and s/he may win. (*EVE Online* player)

One of our interviewees insightfully observed that when the task requires a predefined strategy, there is actually no motivation for the players to discuss, negotiate, plan and make decisions. They just go ahead and do the task. On the other hand, it was very interesting to observe the long and multiple-threaded discussions of the members of our *Tribal Wars(R)* tribe on the in-game tribe forum, regarding, for example, the detailed planning and coordination of a raid. *Tribal Wars(R)* do not have any built-in quests but rather player–player or tribe–tribe interactions such as negotiations, diplomacy, wars, alliances, pacts. The flexibility and the affordances of the environment seemed to promote the emergence of a number of different player strategies and meaningful player discourse.

In *Lineage II(R)*, the environment follows the progress of the player: the players can only assume quests that correspond to their level of progress or their class. Despite, though, the different characters, races and classes and the different play styles, all the quests seemed to have a similar format: collection of items or defeating monsters, as opposed to the different levelling approach of *Star Wars Galaxies* as described by Ducheneaut and Moore (2004b) where the virtual characters gain experience by practising the skills of their class (e.g., healers are gaining experience by healing other characters and not by killing monsters). Upon completion of each quest, the players are rewarded with items, in-game currency, experience points that help them progress to the next level and skill points that help them upgrade the skills of their virtual characters and acquire more skills. At predefined intervals, there are more elaborate and sophisticated quests that mark the transfer of a character from one class to another, higher class. The format of these quests is similar to the format of previous quests with an increased, though, level of difficulty and complexity.

Gameplay and game content

Gee (2007, 19) distinguished game play from game content, with game play involving the mechanics and the format of the player tasks and interaction with the environment and content referring mainly to the narrative, the story and the context of the game. This distinction was also supported by our findings, and mainly by the interviews. The players referred to the content or style of the game (e.g., mythological, fantasy, science fiction) and separated it from the game play, as factors influencing their selection of game. When the players were asked to explain what 'gameplay' was to them, they mainly reported the complexity, the depth of play, the variety and the interconnection of tasks in relation to the main context of the game and the interaction of the player with the environment.

Interviewees reported that the gameplay and the narrative were actually more sophisticated in single-player games than in multiplayer games and attributed this mainly to the design limitations and the nature of an MMOG:

> Usually, single player games have more depth and a more expanded storyline than multi-player games. Multi-player games are usually like this: go, shot and leave. (*Lineage II* player)

> [The narrative] of single player games is more intense. And that's because single player games are usually based on already existing books. (*Lineage II* player)

> If the game has a good story, it's like reading a book; but this doesn't usually happen in multi-player games. Especially lately, games have turned to this direction: to be an interactive book. You choose how the story will evolve. [For multi-player games] it's difficult to have 100,000 people and each one of them

to try to choose [how the story will evolve]. (*Tribal Wars*, *DotA*, *Age of Conan* and *The West* player)

The game content and game play are dynamic and evolving both due to their social aspect and the interactions among the players, as well as regarding their technical development. The content of most popular games such as *EVE Online(R)*, *WoW* and *Lineage II(R)* is considerably different now than when they were first released. Game design had to facilitate the players of the early years to explore as much content as possible and familiarise themselves with its functions. The progress of the players during the course of years and the establishment of a standard in-game population entailed the evolution of the game. The games are updated through periodic expansions the players have to install, so as to keep the interest of more advanced players raised. New players now have to cope with a different environment and the raised game demands rather than the early years' new players, since both the design of the game as well as the average level of the other players have evolved:

> Some time back things were different. Level 60 was the highest. It was different. Now it's more serious I would say. It's more difficult, yes. (*WoW* player)

The narrative

The narrative and the story background of the game constitute factors for the immersion of the players we interviewed into the game world – features that can be traced back to the early pen-and-paper role-playing games, predecessors of MMORPGs. The references to the background story of the game are extensive on the official sites of most MMOGs: the 'Backstory' of *EVE Online(R)*, the 'Legend' of *Lineage II(R)*, the 'Lore' of the *WoW*.

The tasks, the affordances of the environment, the characters and their skills are meaningfully integrated into this narrative. In *EVE Online(R)*, for example, the skills each character race has are relevant to their background and storyline: the *Calende* race, the democrats, have higher memory and intelligence; these skills provide them with the potential to take up tasks such as logistics and manipulation of specific in-game items.

An interesting issue that emerged in our research was that a number of interviewees have compared aspects of their ideology to specific game background aspects relating, in this way, with the narrative context of the environment, an issue that probably requires further research:

> [...] and naturally, due to my personality and ideology, I selected a democrat character. (*EVE Online* player)

> [I was] in the Alliance. I had to be. As a mentality, though, I would rather be in the Horde. But I had to be with the Alliance because my friends were also there. (*WoW* player)

Characters and roles

In most MMOGs, the players may select their avatar from a range of virtual characters. Each character has different skills and a different role in the game. Characters, furthermore, in some games, such as the *WoW*, may be assigned to different professions, such as a blacksmith, a tailor, a fisherman or an engineer, forming an economic system and what was described by Ducheneaut and Moore (2004b) as an 'ecology of professions'. Even in web-based MMOGs where there is no option to select an avatar, players assume different roles such as a 'defensive', 'offensive' or a 'mixed' villages player as in the case of *Tribal Wars*, where the players may decide on the orientation of their play style. The character selected defines the mode of gameplay. In games such as *Lineage II(R)* and *WoW*, the main character archetypes are the fighters and the mages. The fighters possess the power and strength to cope with combats, and the mages have the ability to cast spells and restore power and health on other characters, while in *EVE Online(R)* the race defines the fighting or managerial skills of the character.

In some cases, as indicated by our interviews, the players are attached to their virtual characters. They invest time and effort in selecting their race or class, appearance and skills. They follow the progress of their characters taking screenshots of their different characters' levels and they feel pride and satisfaction through this progress:

> [...] When you name a character, you get attached. It becomes like your pet. You take it home and then it doesn't leave. (*Lineage II* player)

> [...] the characters I create... I take care of them, since they are my creations; I don't select a random name. I think about it [...]. I mean, I personally want my characters to represent something. [...] You love it. During the game, you feel as if it's your creation. You child, let's say. (*WoW* player)

It was also reported by our interviewees that the variety of characters available sustains their interest. They commented that lack of character variety would render the game 'boring':

> I can't imagine a MMO society where they will all be like ants. If they are all the same [...] it wouldn't be an interesting society, I guess. (*WoW* player)

During our ethnographic study, it was observed that the majority of players had created more than one virtual character (Ducheneaut and Moore 2004a): the 'main' and the 'alts', as described in the *WoW* jargon. It seems that the possibility to play with more than one character in one game account keeps the players coming back to the game to try new roles. Through a different character, the players discover different aspects of the game such as new skills, quests and tasks.

When the players were asked, during the interviews, about the purpose of the diversity of characters, real-life references came up more than once:

They offer what the electrician or the cook etc offer in real-life. Each one in his/her own field. (*Lineage II* player)

That is why the game is simply unique. Because there are a lot of players, a lot of characters, a lot of different people, trying to cooperate with each other. It's like a big company or a department of a company. (*WoW* player)

Each character has different skills, which, as mentioned earlier, support the economic circle as well as the levelling up objective of the game. It is impossible to progress in the game without taking advantage of the skills of other characters and players. 'They protect each other', a 17-year-old *Lineage II(R)* player commented:

When everybody's skills are the same, there is no point in being with anyone else, since you can do the same things yourself. (*Lineage II* player)

At this point, we distinguish the skills of the virtual characters, such as the skill to craft objects or to resist a fight, from the real-life skills of the player, such as the strategy, the patience and the perception, both essential for the gaming experience. The knowledge is distributed between the virtual character and the real player (Gee 2007, 77). It is the balanced combination of both that constitutes an effective unit.

It is not only the skills of each character that define their role in the game, though. If the players are members of a group, they take up additional roles, assigned by the group. Our interviewees reported that in-game skills as well as real-life personality traits are the main selection criteria for the assignment of roles in a group. Further discussion on this point will follow in the section concerning the group structure and formation.

From sociability to cooperation and collaboration

The social aspect of gaming seems to be one of the most motivating aspects of MMOGs, as discussed in the section on motivation. The players are among other players, they interact and communicate with other real people through the communication channels available. They are, most of the time, surrounded by chatter as Ducheneaut et al. (2006) noted, especially in areas such as towns, peaceful zones, where players are gathered to trade, upgrade their skills, rest, craft items. The design of these areas favours socialisation, as Raph Koster noted in his post on Socialization and Convenience (Raph Koster's website: http://www.raphkoster.com/2009/01/28/ways-to-make-your-virtual-space-more-social/#more-2486). What we would be looking for, though, in an educational environment, beyond the social interactions, is the constructive and meaningful cooperation and collaboration among participants. The presence of other players does not necessarily lead to meaningful grouping and collaboration. Players may perceive others as a means for developing a better image for their avatars and themselves or simply as an audience for their achievements (Ducheneaut et al. 2006). How can the environment promote and support such constructive and meaningful interactions and what are the types of interactions emerging? Nardi and Harris (2006) described the collaborative interactions in *WoW* that range from 'random acts of fun' where the players engage in socialising activities, such as dancing or flirting, to the well-structured interactions of a guild or a party, with clear objectives and strategies. We tried to get an insight of the motivations and objectives of the players behind these interactions as well as the affordances of the environment that promote or discourage such interactions.

Although most of the MMOGs allow for single-player gaming in the environment, interaction with other players is essential, if the player wants to take advantage of the full potential of the game and explore its content. In higher levels, in particular, with higher stakes quests and tasks, cooperation is essential. Interaction among different virtual characters is also essential, as discussed in the previous section on the different characters and roles.

A design technique employed by certain games such as the *WoW* and the *Aion(R)*,[9] as an initial step for the establishment of cooperation – and competition – is the categorisation of the characters into allying and opposing races. As came up in our interviews, this categorisation leads to the emergence of a sense of solidarity and duty among the allying races. A 29-year-old male *WoW* player commented:

> It has to do mainly with the sense of team, and it's funny, because people that don't even know each other, with nothing in common except of the race, consider it as their duty to defend the new players being killed by someone else.

The sense of affinity seems to add to the emergence of collaborative interactions, as also discussed by Rauterberg (2003). The players can see each other's avatar, they can gesture, they can meet in designated areas, such as the 'clan halls' in *Lineage II(R)*, they can develop their own friend lists with people they have met and enjoyed interacting with. Shared social space increases cooperative behaviour and readiness to form coalitions (Rauterberg 2003).

Peer mentoring also constitutes a critical factor, which came up in all our interviews and was observed during our participation in the games. Peer mentoring can be either structured: through, for example, the 'academies' of *Lineage II(R)*, incubators for new clan members to random acts of more experienced players helping and supporting novice players. And in return, the novice players are expected to help other novice players. The complexity of a game, and in some cases the competitive nature, may discourage new players. At this point, the support of a group, such as a 'clan', a 'guild' or a 'tribe', or even the support of random helping strangers is decisive for the progress of the new player:

> I got to the point that I can also help new players in turn. Like a chain. You have been trained; you know how to train others. (*EVE Online* player)

> I will help them [players asking for help], because when I first started the game, my friends also provided me with gear, outfit, weapons and even helped me with my quests. (*Lineage II* player)

Ducheneaut et al. (2006), though, identified a design feature of the environment that deters lower level players from grouping: lower level players are more focused on levelling up their character through solo playing, before venturing on grouping with other people. Newbie areas are usually void of other players, since most of the players have already achieved higher levels and frequent in more advanced areas of the environment. If we are looking at a learning environment, participation of the players in groups and practice of communication and collaboration skills as early as possible would possibly be a desirable feature.

The essentiality of collaboration is established by specific activities that the player may only accomplish with the cooperation of one or more people or as a member of a 'clan' or of an 'alliance'. In *Lineage II(R)*, for example, the task for acquiring a specific type of outfit can only be accomplished if the player has the support of a 'sponsor' to oversee the quest and pay a fee to an NPC; the sieges of castles can only be assumed by alliances; 'raid boss' quests can only be accomplished by a party of players. Failure to a task that can only be tackled by a group may lead to the death of the character and consequently the loss of experience points, items and adena – the in-game currency of *Lineage II(R)*. Such penalties prevent the player from venturing into more sophisticated tasks alone, similar to the impact of the severe death penalty impact on cooperation among players discussed by Yee (2008).

The economy system of the games, especially the MMORPGs, requires a constant interaction with other characters. The characters coordinate their skills and resources to attain a goal. A character, for example, with the skill to collect items, requires the cooperation of another character with the skill to manufacture objects with these items, and a character with the skill to trade the manufactured objects with other characters, which, in turn, require these objects in order to progress. This diversity of characters and skills seems to form a type of economic chain, very similar to the structure of real-life society.

It is not uncommon that players join the game and play together with their real-life friends or form personal relations with players they meet online. In many cases, close friendships, real-life romances and even real-life marriages were reported among players both in our interviews as well as on game-related fora (WoW Player Stories: http://www.worldofwarcraft.com/community/stories/stories.xml). As some of our interviewees reported:

> I have made two friends through *WoW*. I truly consider them friends. […] I have friends abroad, but we don't talk that often. Because, first of all, we don't share the everyday life and the same experiences. (*WoW* player)

> I feel as if I am entering a different world. Instead of going out with my friends, I log in with my friends. (*Lineage II* player)

Competition

Competition also seems to be a strong motivator for the engagement in the game (Bartle 1996; Yee 2006b). Competing with others was also reported as one of the most predominant activities of players in our interviews. Player competition affordances, therefore, are quite common in most MMOGs, with designated areas such as the PvP servers in *Lineage II(R)* and *WoW* or the 'low-security' areas in *EvE Online(R)*, where the players can engage in PvP combats. Competition, in some cases, is also encouraged through the introduction of opposing races, as mentioned in the previous section on cooperation. In *WoW*, for instance, the player may select from two opposing races: the 'Alliance' and the 'Horde' and in *Aion(R)*, between the 'Elyos' and the 'Asmodians'. By condition, the members of these two races are enemies. There is, in effect, no verbal communication between these opposing races. Members of one race cannot understand the 'language' of the other. If, for example, a Horde player types in the chat channel the word 'LOL' (laughing out loud), the Alliance members will see something entirely different such as 'KEK', thus eliminating the possibility for inter-racial verbal communication. Although we cannot support this with empirical data, there are indications that this differentiation of virtual characters affects the players' behaviour in the game. The representation of an avatar seems to have an impact on the behaviour of the player (Yee and Bailenson 2007), an issue that also came up in our interviews and our ethnographic study.

Even in such cases though, competition among players has specific rules, in order to prevent abuse of power over lower level, novice players or offensive language and behaviour. Specific rules are set by the game and the game administrators so as to prevent aggression and violence through functions such as designated 'peaceful' and 'safe' areas, the possibility to report abuse with severe penalties for the offenders or the labelling of a player as 'chaotic' (in *Lineage II*), entailing the inability to perform specific actions in the game. Aggressive behaviour is also discouraged by a large number of players, isolating, in this way, players that tend to transcend the limits of 'fair play' or the social norms agreed among players (see also Myers 2008).

Communication

The main built-in communication medium in MMOGs is the text-based chat or the fora. Text communication is usually realised through a chat window and via different channels: a player can chat with another player character through private messages, 'shout' so as to be heard by all players within a certain distance, communicate only with members of their own group or block messages from specific players. Text communication, though, is not enough in most of the games, especially in cases where quick communication is needed, such as during combat, or when more elaborate information exchange or discussion is required. In these cases, players either develop codes for fast text communication or use external VoIP (Voice over Internet Protocol) communication tools. VoIP could also be a way for decreasing, in some cases, cognitive overload of players (Nelson and Erlandson 2008). Through voice communication, the members of a group develop stronger links with other group members (Williams, Caplan, and Xiong 2007). Some of our interviewees also reported that they resort to voice communication to strengthen the sense of awareness among members. There were, on the other hand, cases of players preferring to use voice communication only when required by the task (Williams et al. 2006).

Although literature suggests that written communication is linked to careful and critical thinking and reflection (Garrison, Anderson, and Archer 1999), the fast-paced nature of the communication via chat in games does not seem to provide the affordances for elaborate discussions. In the web-based game *Tribal Wars(R)*, though, where asynchronous communication via the tribe forum is the main integrated communication channel, we had several opportunities to observe long discussions, exchange of opinions, disagreements, negotiation, decision-making and planning among the members of the group (see example in Table 2). Communication structures supporting high-level questions and explanations constitute factors with a positive impact on collaborative problem-solving and learning (Webb 1989; Hoppe and Ploetzner 1999). Different communication affordances and channels in a gaming environment may contribute to the emergence of reflective skills and collaborative learning.

Communication affordances and channels though do not seem to suffice for the emergence of higher order thinking and meaningful discourse. As discussed in the task-design section, the flexibility of the environment and the possibility to select from a range of different approaches for attaining a goal increases the potential for discourse among players. In *Tribal Wars(R)*, the majority of the time between battles is spent on discussions about the best possible strategies, tips to new players and even social chat. Players of MMOGs, such as *Lineage II(R)*, *WoW* and *EVE Online(R)*, interviewed during our research situated discussions within the context of open-ended tasks such as decisions for the future orientation and goals of the group, the acceptance or dismissal of members and the participation or not to specific quests.

The groups

Although there are different types of groups in an MMOG, such as parties, clans, alliances, raids, as also described by Nardi and Harris (2006), in our

Table 2. Excerpt from a *Tribal Wars* tribe forum.

V. 11-03 19:44	Hit reset …
P. 11-03 19:46	Somewhere close to K22. I will fill you up with resources! There are plenty of us out there now.
V. 11-03 19:58	Listen to the Teacher!!! You will also be of better help for the tribe there …
K. 11-03 20:03	As I said in the other thread, she can't choose a continent. Just an orientation and this is risky because of the distances!!!
P. 11-03 20:49	Come on! You play Tribal Wars for so long and you haven't befriended an admin yet? They'll just hit a button and she'll be in the centre of the tribe! I think you should send a letter ..! :ppp
K. 11-03 20:59	There is an option for those already in a Tribe and loose their villages, when they reset, they just select the option to appear again in the centre of their tribe!!!
PL. 11-03 21:06	What r u talking about? Super!! It will be just fine here, there are quite a few small attacks around … hmmm … maybe I should reset, myself?
KL. 11-03 21:06	You must be joking
LT. 11-03 21:10	[To PL.] you stay where you are :p
PL. 11-03 21:10	No!!! I just want to enjoy the game! The big ones won't bag me any more! I made my decision! Reset!
Ki. 11-03 21:11	What if we all restarted? Can you imagine what would happen?
LT. 11-03 21:12	… funeral XD
Ki. 11-03 21:06	Absolutely right!!!

Note: Discussion about the location of one of the Tribe members. Only the initials of the player's pseudonyms have been kept, for protecting anonymity of the players.

interviews, the players seemed to identify only their 'clans', 'guilds', 'corporations' or 'tribes' as legitimate groups because of the more organised structure, commitment and responsibility required by group members, as opposed to the ephemeral and random nature of the parties and smaller groups of people:

> The 'party' is not a group. A group is the 'clan'. The party is considered as a friendly company. I don't think that the 'party' is a group. (*Lineage II* player)

> [in a party] you don't really care about your stats, because you will probably never see these people again. (*WoW* player)

There are a number of different techniques for the formation of a group: for the random parties, the players may use the integrated in-game functions, such as the 'autofixing' of a group from random interested players or the 'group matching', or simply by 'shouting' at the chat channel available to all players in nearby areas. The size of these groups varies according to the specific quest pursued. In order to find a structured group, though, such as the 'guild' or 'clan', the player will have to follow specific procedures.

These structured groups vary in size, structure, composition and goals. There are groups specialising in PvP activities, PvE activities, manufacturing of items or mixed activities, international or language-specific groups, groups focused on levelling up or groups simply for socialising and having fun. Their common objective, though, is the protection and support of the members of the group, so as for the members to support and strengthen the group in turn, as one of our interviewees commented.

Although Ducheneaut et al. (2006) observed that grouping was an inefficient method for levelling up and characters would group mainly for accessing content that would otherwise be impossible or difficult to access, during our ethnographic immersion and our discussions with the interviewees, we encountered cases of groups specifically oriented to lower level players or players who admitted that without the support of their group they would not have been able to progress as fast. In *Tribal Wars(R)*, a novice player with only one village in his/her possession may easily become prey to neighbouring, more advanced players, without the support of a group – support consisted of resources, troops and advice. There are indications, therefore, that the group protects the members from enemy groups, it provides resources and peer-mentoring and it facilitates the progress of the characters. The members are responsible for providing help to other members, when required, and participate in team activities such as the 'raids':

If you are in a group, you are strong. (*EVE Online* player)

[the group] is like a very big company. A department of a company, let's say, where people are trying to cooperate in order to achieve a goal. If you don't cooperate correctly, the goal will not be attained. (*WoW* player)

The need for sociability may be another motivator for grouping. Ducheneaut et al. (2006) concluded that grouping is not significantly affected by the orientation of the server (PvP, PvE or role playing). Players form groups even in the cases where the goals of the game system do not require grouping.

Most games have a built-in structure, such as the 'Royal Guards' in *Lineage II(R)*, forming a type of hierarchy. But additionally to this predefined structure, players tend to develop their own hierarchy structure and ranks, when they feel it is required, such as the 'Academy Manager' in *Lineage II(R)*, the 'Diplomat' in *Tribal Wars(R)*, the 'Class Officer' in *WoW*. Players who have the real-life skills and have gained the respect and trust of the leader and other group members are usually assigned to these ranks. It is in most cases this 'elite' together with the leader who are responsible for setting the rules and making the decisions in the group.

The group leader is usually the founder and defines the orientation and objectives of the group. When the interviewees were asked about the features of a good leader, they mostly referred to the real-life skills of the player, such as communication skills, intuitiveness, interest in the game, the group and the members, to be able to impose discipline and direct the group:

> I believe that the guild master has to spend three times more the time of other players. It's a tremendously time-consuming process. You have to take care of everything. [...] in many cases, the guild master is a typical example, because it requires maturity. He can't be 15 years old and be able to complete a serious raid, be a serious raiding guild. You have to have experience of the game. You have to have maturity. A typical example of guild master is someone who has played for many years. (29-year-old *WoW* player)

In cases of small groups, the role of the leader seems to be slightly altered, as one of our interviewees commented:

> In most of the cases, in my experience, in small groups, the role of the leader is somewhat nominal, since all the group members are equal – at least when they are at the same level. Sometimes, though, he/she has to sort out disagreements among the members. (*WoW* player)

The new members are usually selected according to different criteria for each group: the personality, the level and gear of the character, the language, and the skills. In some cases, players have to fill in extensive application forms for joining a group:

> It is like filling up a job application! (*WoW* player)

Most of our interviewees reported that usually new members have to go through a trial period in order for their compatibility with the group to be tested. If the new member does not comply with the rules or respect other group members, s/he is usually dismissed. The process for accepting new members in a guild is also linked to the stronger relationships among group members (Williams et al. 2006) – thorough processes for admitting new members seem to increase consensus in the group and strengthen the relationships among the members.

Communication and collaboration came up, during the interviews, as the more critical features of a good group. In an effective group, the players know their role, they feel responsible for each other, they accept failure well, without internal conflicts, they have fun together and often develop personal relations with each other, knowing each other with their real-life names and with a good balance between the progress of the group and its social aspect. An effective group is also a balanced group, with different race or class characters so as to take advantage of all the different skills available. Other factors for strengthening the bonding of the group are the collective activities (Ducheneaut et al. 2006), the social chat even that which is personal or irrelevant to the game topics, trust, personal contact among the players – factors that were also reported by players in our interviews – and also the size of the group: the larger is the group, the more difficult it is to bond with all its members (Ducheneaut et al. 2006).

Decision-making also varies from group to group, ranging from leader-oriented and authoritarian to more democratic, through conversation and voting:

> I was, initially, impressed by the fact that the guilds in *WoW* are not at all democratic, as a process, as authority and how this authority is distributed. And I had some arguments against it, in a philosophical base mainly. But, in reality, the soul of the guild is the guild leader [...]. S/he spends three times more the time anyone else is spending in the game [...]. S/he has to take care of everything. (*WoW* player)

> We elect the leader, the president in our corporation, based on our statute. (*EVE Online* player).

Although structured groups – guilds, clans or tribes – seem to play a predominant role in the gaming experience of the players, they seem to be 'fragile institutions' (Ducheneaut et al. 2006). Most of our interviewees reported that they have shifted from one group to another more than once because they would disagree with the practices of the group, the group would not match their objectives or because of personal conflicts. 'When the group loses its vision and does not fulfil the members' expectations, is bound to fail', as one of our interviewees commented. Commitment to the group is higher when the members spend time playing together and form stronger relationships (Seay et al. 2004).

Conclusions and limitations

Massively multiplayer online games have been criticised for their violent content, their addictive effects and the aggression of character against character. Nevertheless, their intrinsic motivation, the networks of interaction and communication emerging within and beyond the game with the development of player-created content and online communities, and the increasing player population has shifted them to the focus of research in areas such as education, sociology and communication. Their design actively engages players and sustains their interest, while it promotes and supports multiple forms of interaction in and beyond the game.

This study sought to investigate the potential of MMOGs for the emergence of collaborative learning through a conceptual framework based on constructivist learning approaches, collaborative problem-solving and computer-mediated communication research. Our framework was based on two central axes: the task design and the interactions affordances design, two elements that seemed to be interconnected and interrelated within a functional virtual environment. We described the factors relevant to the support of learning and the acquisition of knowledge through collaborative interactions that could inform the design of effective tasks and interaction affordances. We hypothesised that inherent features of MMOGs, such as the integrated goal-oriented tasks and the affordances for meaningful interactions among players, would scaffold opportunities for collaborative problem-solving and we attempted to test this framework on existing massively multiplayer games.

These two elements were also the main motivators, as reported by our interviewees. The design of the environment, the narrative, the depth of play, the different virtual characters and the social aspect of gaming constitute decisive factors for the immersion of the player in the environment. The personalisation of the gameplay, the identification of the player with different aspects of the environment and the integration of activities and tasks into a meaningful context are features that attract and sustain the participation of the players and also scaffold their interactions.

Two categories of skills and knowledge seemed to emerge from the interaction of the PvE: game-related knowledge and skills and interpersonal skills such as communication and negotiation. Game-related knowledge is supported by the design of the tasks and distributed between the players, the environment and external to the game resources, while interpersonal skills can also be supported by the design of the tasks as well as by the cooperative or competitive interactions among players. Knowledge emerges through extensive practice with the environment and through the communication and collaboration with other players. Players ask for help from others or help other players, negotiate terms of pacts, combats or behaviour, and conduct within and beyond a group; they form larger or smaller groups, communicate for reaching a decision and collaborate for attaining shared goals. Meaningful, domain-specific and transferable to real-life knowledge could be promoted through the integration of the appropriate content. With the exploitation of the game design elements that support learning, peer-interaction and constructive competition, and their application into an appropriate narrative and story, MMOG environments can constitute effective collaborative learning environments. The fantasy narrative structure and the story are definitive of the learning attributes of games as they can convey 'social' and 'academic' goals of a game, instead of 'violent' and 'commercial' ones and they can also 'make complex phenomena approachable' (Young 2004).

The requirements of the environment tasks in combination with the requirements of players for socialisation and for interaction with a dynamic and flexible content were at the basis of cooperative and competitive interactions. Design features such as the underlying economy system, tasks requiring the formation of partnerships and alliances, and mechanisms for strengthening consensus and links among group members may promote the role of the group as an effective unit in the gaming experience. Interpersonal and communication skills may be supported by appropriate task design, communication affordances and channels for the promotion of discussions, argumentation, negotiation and decision-making, skills that are essential for collaborative problem-solving and learning.

The findings and conclusions of this study are not definitive and conclusive. They were based on data from ethnographic research and on self-reports from a rather small sample of interviews that were not representative of the player population. We cannot, therefore, extrapolate our results to the design of all MMOGs nor to the larger players' population, but we believe that they may offer important insights and implications for research on the educational perspective of MMOGs. Further research through comparative content analysis and from gameplay datasets could inform the instructional design of effective virtual collaborative learning environments.

Acknowledgements

With thanks to the *Lineage II* team of *NCSoft Europe* and to *Beacon Mutlimedia*, distributors in Greece, and particularly to Mr Christian Vestøl and Mr Dimitris Pavlis for their interest in our research and their support. Also, many thanks to the anonymous reviewers for their very knowledgeable and constructive comments, and to all the players who participated in our research for their time and their passionate, insightful and encouraging comments.

Notes

1. *World of Warcraft*. http://www.worldofwarcraft.com/index.xml.
2. *Lineage II*. http://www.lineage2.com/.
3. *Left4Dead*. http://www.14d.com/.
4. *Tribal Wars*. http://www.fyletikesmaxes.gr/.
5. *The West*. http://www.the-west.net/.
6. *EVE Online*. http://www.eveonline.com/.
7. *DotA*. http://www.dota-allstars.com/.
8. *Age of Conan*. http://www.ageofconan.com/.
9. *Aion*. http://na.aiononline.com/.

References

Anderson, J. 1980. *Cognitive psychology and its implications*. San Francisco: Freeman.

Atkinson, R., C. McBeath, D. Jonas-Dwyer, and R. Phillips. 2004. Beyond the comfort zone. Paper presented at the 21st ASCILITE Conference, ed. R. Atkinson, C. McBeath, D. Jonas-Dwyer, and R. Phillips, December 5–8, in Perth.

Bartle, R.A. 1996. Hearts, clubs, diamonds, spades: Players who suit muds. *Journal of MUD Research* 1, no. 1. http://www.mud.co.uk/richard/hcds.htm.

Csikszentmihalyi, M. 1992. *Flow: The classic work on how to achieve happiness.* New York: Harper Perennial.
De Freitas, S. 2009. Massively multiplayer online role-play games for learning. In *Handbook of research on effective electronic gaming in education,* ed. R.E. Ferdig, 51–66. Hershey, PA: IGI Global.
Dibbell, J. 2007. The life of the Chinese gold farmer. *New York Times,* June 17, Magazine. http://www.nytimes.com/2007/06/17/magazine/17lootfarmers-t.html
Dickey, M.D. 2007. Game design and learning: A conjectural analysis of how massively multiple online role-playing games (MMORPGs) foster intrinsic motivation. *Educational Technology Research and Development* 55, no 3: 253–73.
Dillenbourg, P. 1999. What do you mean by collaborative learning? In *Collaborative-learning: Cognitive and computational approaches,* ed. P. Dillenbourg, 1–19. Oxford: Elsevier.
Ducheneaut, N., and R.J. Moore. 2004a. 'Let me get my alt': Digital identiti(es) in multiplayer games. Paper presented at the CSCW 2004 Workshop on Representation of Digital Identities, November 6, in Chicago.
Ducheneaut, N., and R.J. Moore. 2004b. The social side of gaming: A study of interaction patterns in a massively multiplayer online game. Paper presented at the ACM Conference on Computer Supported Cooperative Work, November 6–10, in Chicago.
Ducheneaut, N., N. Yee, E. Nickell, and R.J. Moore. 2006. 'Alone together?' Exploring the social dynamics of massively multiplayer online games. Paper presented at the ACM conference on Human Factors in computing systems – CHI 2006, April 22–27, in Montreal.
Frensch, P.A., and R.J. Sternberg. 1991. Skill-related differences in game playing. *Complex problem solving: Principles and mechanisms,* ed. R.J. Sternberg and P.A. Frensch, 343–81. Hillsdale, NJ: Lawrence Erlbaum.
Galarneau, L. 2005. Spontaneous communities of learning: A social analysis of learning ecosystems in massively multiplayer online gaming (MMOG) environments. Paper presented at the Digital Games Research Association (DiGRA) Conference, June 16–20, in Vancouver.
Garrison, D.R., T. Anderson, and W. Archer. 1999. Critical inquiry in a text-based environment: Computer conferencing in higher education. *The Internet and Higher Education* 2, nos. 2–3: 87–105.
Gee, J.P. 2003. *What video games have to teach us about learning and literacy.* New York: Palgrave Macmillan.
Gee, J.P. 2004. Learning by design: Games as learning machines. *Interactive Educational Multimedia* 8: 15–23.
Gee, J.P. 2007. *Good video games and good leaning: Collected essays on video games, learning and literacy. New literacies and digital epistemologies.* New York: Peter Lang.
Hämäläinen R., T. Manninen, S. Järvelä, and P. Häkkinen. 2006. Learning to collaborate: Designing collaboration in a 3-D game environment. *The Internet and Higher Education* 9, no. 1: 47–61.
Hine, C. 2000. *Virtual ethnography.* Thousand Oaks, CA: Sage.
Hoppe, H.U., and P.R. Ploetzner. 1999. Can analytic models support learning in groups? In *Collaborative-learning: Cognitive and computational approaches,* ed. P. Dillenbourg (Advances in Learning and Instruction Series), 147–69. Oxford: Elsevier.

Huffaker, D., J.A. Wang, J. Treem, M.A. Ahmad, L. Fullerton, D. Williams, M.S. Poole, et al. 2009. The social behaviors of experts in massive multiplayer online role-playing games. Paper presented at the 12th IEEE International Conference on Computational Science and Engineering, August 29–31, Vancouver.

Jonassen, D.H. 2000. Toward a design theory of problem solving. *Educational Technology Research and Development* 48, no. 4: 63–85.

Juul, J. 2007. Without a goal – On open and expressive games. In *Videogame, player, text*, ed. B. Atkins and T. Krzywinka, 191–203. Manchester: Manchester University Press.

Kafai, Y. 1994. *Minds in play: Computer game design as a context, for children's learning*. Hillsdale, NJ: Lawrence Erlbaum.

Kiili, K. 2005. Content creation challenges and flow experience in educational games: The IT-Emperor case. *The Internet and Higher Education* 8, no. 3: 183–98.

Lave, J., and E. Wenger. 1991. *Situated learning: Legitimate peripheral participation*. New York: Cambridge University Press.

Lazzaro, N. 2004. Why we play games: Four keys to more emotion in player experiences. Paper presented at the Game Developers Conference, March 24–27, in San Jose, CA. http://www.xeodesign.com/xeodesign_whyweplaygames.pdf and http://archive.gdconf.com/gdc_2004/.

Manninen, T., and T. Kujanpää. 2005. The hunt for collaborative war gaming – Case: Battlefield 1942. *Game Studies: The International Journal of Computer Game Research* 5, no. 1. http://www.gamestudies.org/0501/manninen_kujanpaa/

Mayer, R.E. 1992. *Thinking, problem solving, cognition*. 2nd ed. New York: W.H. Freeman.

Mayer, R.E. 1998. Cognitive, metacognitive, and motivational aspects of problem solving. *Instructional Science* 26, no. 49: 49–63.

Meredith, A., Z. Hussain, and M. Griffiths. 2009. Online gaming: A scoping study of massively multi-player online role playing games. *Electronic Commerce Research* 9, nos. 1–2: 3–26.

Myers, D. 2007. Self and selfishness in online social play. In *Situated Play: Proceedings of DiGRA 2007 Conference*, 226–34. Tokyo: Digital Games Research Association.

Myers, D. 2008. Play and punishment: The sad and curious case of Twixt. In *The [Player] Conference Proceedings*, 1–25. Copenhagen: The Center for Computer Games Research, The IT University of Copenhagen.

Nardi, B., and J. Harris. 2006. Strangers and friends: Collaborative play in World of Warcraft. In *Proceedings of the Conference on Computer-Supported Cooperative Work*, 149–58. New York: ACM Press.

Nelson, B.C., and B.E. Erlandson. 2008. Managing cognitive load in educational multi-user virtual environments: Reflection on design practice. *Educational Technology Research and Development* 56, nos. 5–6: 619–41.

Norton, P., and K.M. Wiburg. 2003. *Teaching with technology: Designing opportunities to learn*. 2nd ed. Belmont, CA: Wadsworth/Thomson Learning.

Prensky, M. 2001. *Digital game-based learning*. New York: McGraw-Hill.

Rauterberg, M. 2003. Determinantes for collaboration in networked multi-user games. *Entertainment computing – Technologies and applications*, ed. R. Nakatsu and J. Hoshino, 313–21. Dordrecht: Kluwer Academic.

Reeves, S., B. Brown, and E. Laurier. 2009. Experts at play: Understanding skilled expertise. *Games and Culture* 4, no. 3: 205–27.

Salen, K., and E. Zimmerman. 2005. Game design and meaningful play. *Handbook of computer game studies*, ed. J. Raessens and J. Goldstein, 59–80. Cambridge, MA: MIT Press.

Schrader, P.G., and M. McCreery. 2008. The acquisition of skill and expertise in massively multiplayer online games. *Educational Technology Research and Development* 56, nos. 5–6: 557–74.

Seay, A.F., W.J. Jerome, K.S. Lee, and R.E. Kraut. 2004. Project massive: A study of online gaming communities. In *Proceedings of the 2004 Conference on Human Factors and Computing Systems – CHI '04*, 1421–4. Vienna: ACM Press.

Stapleton, A.J., and P.C. Taylor. 2003. Why videogames are cool and school sucks! Paper presented at Australian Game Developers Conference, November 20–23, in Melbourne.

Steinkuehler, C.A. 2003. Massively multiplayer online videogames as a constellation of literacy practices. Paper presented at the 2003 International Conference on Literacy, September 22–27, in Ghent, Belgium.

Steinkuehler, C.A. 2004a. Learning in massively multiplayer online games. Paper presented at the 6th international conference on Learning Sciences, June 22–26, at Santa Monica, CA, 521–8.

Steinkuehler, C.A. 2004b. Online cognitive ethnography: Methods for studying massively multiplayer online video gaming culture. Paper presented at the 17th annual conference on Interdisciplinary Qualitative Studies, January 9–11, in Athens, GA.

Steinkuehler, C.A. 2006. Why game (culture) studies now? *Games and Culture* 1, no. 1: 97–102.

Steinkuehler, C.A., and D. Williams. 2006. Where everybody knows your (screen) name: Online games as 'third places'. *Journal of Computer-Mediated Communication* 11, no. 4: 885–909.

Voulgari, I., and V. Komis. 2008. Massively multi-user online games: The emergence of effective collaborative activities for learning. Poster paper presented at the 2nd IEEE International Conference on Digital Game and Intelligent Toy Enhanced Learning, November 17–19, in Banff, Canada.

Webb, N. 1989. Peer interaction and learning in small groups. *International Journal of Educational Research* 13: 21–39.

Williams, D., S. Caplan, and L. Xiong. 2007. Can you hear me now? The impact of voice in an online gaming community. *Human Communication Research* 33, no. 4: 427–49.

Williams, D., N. Ducheneaut, L. Xiong, Y. Zhang, N. Yee, and E. Nickell. 2006. From tree house to barracks: The social life of guilds in World of Warcraft. *Games and Culture* 1, no. 4: 338–61.

Yee, N. 2006a. Motivations for play in online games. *Cyberpsychology & Behavior: The Impact of the Internet, Multimedia and Virtual Reality on Behavior and Society* 9, no. 6: 772–5.

Yee, N. 2006b. The labor of fun: How video games blur the boundaries of work and play. *Games and Culture* 1, no. 1: 68–71.

Yee, N. 2008. *Social architectures in MMOs*. http://www.nickyee.com/daedalus/archives/print/001625.php

Yee, N., and J. Bailenson. 2007. The proteus effect: The effect of transformed self-representation on behavior. *Human Communication Research* 33: 271–90.

Young, M. 2004. An ecological description of videogames in education. Paper presented at the annual conference on Education and Information Systems: Technologies and Applications, July 21–25, in Orlando, FL.

Young, M., P.G. Schrader, and D. Zheng. 2006. MMOGs as learning environments: An ecological journey into Quest Atlantis and the Sims Online. *Innovate: Journal of online education* 2, no. 4. http://www.innovateonline.info/index.php?view=article&id=66

Serious playground: using *Second Life* to engage high school students in urban planning

Kerry Mallan[a], Marcus Foth[b], Ruth Greenaway[a] and Greg T. Young[b]

[a]School of Cultural and Language Studies in Education, Queensland University of Technology, Kelvin Grove, Brisbane, Australia; [b]Urban Informatics Research Lab, Institute for Creative Industries and Innovation, Queensland University of Technology, Kelvin Grove, Brisbane, Australia

> Virtual world platforms such as *Second Life* have been successfully used in educational contexts to motivate and engage learners. This article reports on an exploratory workshop involving a group of high school students using *Second Life* for an urban planning project. Young people are traditionally an under-represented demographic when it comes to participating in urban planning and decision-making processes. The research team developed activities that combined technology with a constructivist approach to learning. Real-world experiences and purposes ensured that the workshop enabled students to see the relevance of their learning. Our design also ensured that play remained an important part of the learning. By conceiving of the workshop as a 'serious playground', we investigated the ludic potential of learning in a virtual world.

Introduction

In the popular imagination, the word 'virtual' triggers the thought of computers and digital technology, and with it, an imaginary world where we meet friends, take virtual tours, play games and participate in a host of simulated or virtual experiences. Youth are among the highest users of a range of digital technologies and actively participate daily in virtual communities via online network gaming, social networking sites, blogs and email (Buckingham 2000). These virtual environments do not replace other 'real' spaces, but extend and integrate these largely social spaces (Leander and McKim 2003). It is unsurprising that educators are turning their attention to the ways in which virtual or simulated experiences can be used to capitalise on their immersive learning qualities. In navigating a virtual world, there are social as well as expressive (aural, visual, textural and perspectival) cues that characterise the immersive experience. The main immersive feature of virtual worlds is the ability of the user to navigate a space and interact with the people, objects and places, and to influence the course of events as a result (Johnson and Levine 2008, 162). While educators have been exploring the potential of virtual worlds in learning, there has been no reported research on how this technology is being used with high school students in urban design.

This article addresses this gap and reports on an exploratory workshop with a group of high school students using *Second Life* (hereafter, *SL*) as a planning tool for designing a community space as part of an urban redevelopment project. The research is part of a larger project that investigates the way narrative and new media technologies can be utilised in community engagement activities and realised in design ideas. The primary aim of the workshop reported in this article is to test the waters of *SL* as an immersive virtual world for engaging students in learning design and communication skills through play.

Background

Virtual worlds are characterised as computer-generated environments 'that give [...] the user a strong sense of being there' (Warburton 2009, 415). Virtual worlds such as those created through multi-user virtual environments (MUVE), multi-player online games (MMO) and *SL* may appear in different forms, but nevertheless, share a number of common features:

- persistence of the in-world environment;
- a shared space allowing multiple users to participate simultaneously;
- virtual embodiment in the form of an avatar;
- interactions that occur between users and objects in a 3D environment;
- an immediacy of action such that interactions occur in real time; and
- similarities to the real world such as topography, movement and physics that provide the illusion of being there (Smart et al., quoted in Warburton 2009, 415).

Warburton contends that the significant difference between MUVE and MMO is the lack of a predetermined narrative. In *SL*, there is no predetermined purpose (such as winning a quest) unless the user wishes to create or build one. Social interaction in *SL* occurs within an open-ended system that offers the user a number of ways to create content and shape the environment.

Originally developed for gaming, entertainment and recreation purposes, *SL* is now being used extensively in education. Pfeil, Ang and Zaphiris (2009, 225) report that a growing number of UK universities (over 80%) have an *SL* presence, and some are exclusively using *SL* to provide lectures, courses and tutorials to students as well as to tutors. This high usage of *SL* compared with other competing platforms reflects the dominance of this social virtual world platform (Warburton 2009, 416).

In addition to the educational use, there is growing interest among urban designers and planners to use 3D virtual reality models such as *SL* for the design and planning of buildings, neighbourhoods and cities. As a web-based virtual world, *SL* provides opportunities for people to move through and interact with spaces as virtual representations of people (avatars). In *SL*, users can create 3D objects, including social spaces and buildings, thus providing new ways to collaborate in the design of spaces. The city of Boston is recreating parts of Boston in *SL* and includes features such as online concerts and discussion forums to encourage more people to participate in civic life (http://www.planetizen.com/node/25924). They also see this as a way to evaluate proposed new developments in Boston. *Hub2* – an initiative of Emerson College and Boston City Council – is developing teaching resources for the application of 3D virtual technologies as a community engagement tool in urban planning initiatives (Gordon and Koo 2008). Likewise, a group called *Studio Wikitecture* has set up a site in *SL* to co-design a virtual reality health clinic in Nepal (http://nwn.blogs.com/nwn/2008/03/wikitectures-pr.html). The group has also made use of video and photo sharing sites such as *YouTube* and *Flickr* to share the process of designing the building.

The proponents of virtual reality models argue that:

> *SL* allows users to immerse themselves in an environment and engage in synchronous dialogue and production with other graphically represented users. It allows for group authorship, which better enables a sense of collective ownership in a space or object. And unlike professional design programs, it affords users a sense of playfulness and allows them to experiment with designs and concepts that have little connection to empirical reality. (Gordon and Koo 2008, 205)

Furthermore, Gordon and Koo explain that the investment of their time in building a virtual Boston, when the real Boston has so many problems, is justified as, by allowing users the opportunity to build and play in a collaborative environment, *SL* 'has the potential of generating politically viable groups around almost every element of [their] designed world' (Gordon and Koo 2008, 219).

Following on from the work by Gordon and Koo, we designed and conducted an exploratory workshop using *SL* with a group of students from a high school located on the Sunshine Coast of Queensland, Australia (Foth et al. 2009). The following questions informed our workshop:

(1) How could *SL* be used to engage students in an urban planning workshop?

(2) What are the discernible learning experiences afforded by this medium for the students?
(3) In conceiving of *SL* as a game, how does play shape the learning experience?

Theoretical framework

In developing our theoretical framework, we draw on two key notions – constructivist learning and text as game. As our project was not concerned with students' formal learning of curriculum, we wanted to explore the theoretical implications of the informal learning workshop for understanding learning and play as immersive and interactive qualities that *SL* offers with respect to urban design.

Constructivist learning is a pervasive paradigm in research about the existing use of virtual worlds (Dede 1995; Jonassen, Peck, and Wilson 1999). Jonassen, Peck and Wilson argue that constructivism emphasises the student being active in the learning and promotes student-centred learning that supports ownership of the learning experience. Learning should be interesting and relevant and should offer meaningful problems to solve. In designing constructivist learning environments that utilise interactive technologies, researchers and educators include 'cognitive and collaborative tools, various types of scaffolding (conceptual, procedural, metacognitive coaching), and access to resources, models, and exemplars' (Dickey 2005, 441). While we endeavoured to include these considerations in the design of the workshop, time and access constraints meant that we had to work with a reduced set of elements. We expand upon these considerations in our discussion section. An important assumption underpinning our constructivist approach, however, is that students work best when given the opportunity, space and support to collaborate and when faced with tasks that are new and challenging. We also value the role of play as an effective means for motivating the students and encouraging interaction with the objects, space and avatars of the virtual world as well as with other students in the workshop classroom.

Text as game is a way of conceiving *SL* within the workshop. *SL* enables the users to create and construct their own textual world with spontaneous narratives, objects, spatial considerations, interactions, design features, perspectives and rules. The concept of 'game' is prominent in research associated with interactive, experiential and developmental learning, and game theory (Huizinga 1955; Aarseth 1997; Ryan 2001). With the rise of digital cultures and electronic games, the concept has been expanded to include a range of activities, pleasures and forms. While educators have long incorporated games into classroom activities, these institutionalised games, as opposed to free play games, raise a distinction between game and play: games are 'rule bound', whereas play is seen as 'not serious' (Huizinga 1955). Although 'not serious' games do not have a material interest or profit to be gained, they nevertheless absorb the players and promote the formation of social groupings.

In conceiving *SL* as a 'text' and a 'game', we are drawing a parallel with literary theory. Text is a travelling concept that emerged first in literary theory and has since found favour in a range of interdisciplinary studies. In a postmodern sense, text refers not only to written materials but also to film, painting, architecture, information systems and games. In other words, text serves as a way of understanding attempts at representation (Sim 2001, 370). *SL* not only attempts to represent a world that is familiar to the user but also invites ludic activity requiring effort and ingenuity on the part of the user/player. Unlike other texts that are games, *SL* does not offer a problem to be solved by the player. However, we posed a challenge for the students by inviting them to consider how they could design the site that the *SL* platform we had represented with features that could be useful and interesting for the community. Purposefully selected games blended with carefully constructed learning experiences can be used to improve student learning outcomes (Education Queensland 2005). Thus, the workshop specified the goal to be achieved but the purpose was not to win or defeat others. Rather, it was to work collaboratively to make design decisions and to enjoy the learning experience.

Context and setting

The Regional Council, a partner in the grant that supports this study, is redeveloping a site (named Lower Mill Study) that was formerly used as a timber mill. The vision for the new site is 'to develop and sustain facilities […] for present and future generations of the community with balanced consideration to history, culture, education, arts and economics' (http://lowermillsite.com.au/). At this stage, the master plan of the site proposes the development of a new library building as well as the renovation of heritage-listed buildings that formed part of the timber mill precinct (Figure 1). The building of a former butter factory, which has been redesigned as a performing arts centre, is also in close proximity to the site and forms part of the overall master plan. Lower Mill Site will eventually house many community groups and has two 'heritage-listed' buildings from the original sawmill as its centrepiece.

The Council is interested in exploring new ways to engage diverse and traditionally under-represented sections of the local community, such as young people. The objective of our workshops with 20 middle school students, aged 13–15 years, was to experiment with *SL* as an interactive tool to allow them to participate in the project and contribute ideas and feedback for the planned development. The students and their teachers had agreed to participate in planning a heritage journey at the site, and the *SL* workshop was a preliminary and exploratory way of introducing them to the possibilities offered by new media technologies for learning and urban design. (The teachers were invited to

Figure 1. Lower Mill Site.

participate with other adults from the community and the Council at a separate workshop.) Funding for the construction of this heritage journey was provided by the government tourism agency. Ethical clearance and permissions were obtained before proceeding with the *SL* workshop.

Methodology

As noted earlier in this article, the research reported here is based on a small-scale collaborative project between a high school, a regional Council and a team of university researchers, including a doctoral student and a graduate student who designed the *SL* platform for the workshop. The research design for this study is interpretive and qualitative. The use of additional sources of material, such as informal interviews with the students, photographs, design plans and notes taken during the workshop, contributes to the overall data collection and discussion of results.

The approach to qualitative research that characterises this study is closer to the praxis of doing field research, with consideration of integrating theory and analysis in a meaningful and convincing way (Barker 2003). As our workshop participants were young people who were participating in a new learning activity, we wanted to establish a relationship of respectful collaboration between them and the research team. We also wanted to extend this respect to the other adults who participated in the additional *SL* workshop (not reported in this article). Therefore, respect as part of the collaborative nature of the project is an important element of the workshop planning and discussion of results. We consider that our methodological approach reflects an openness and transparency about its interpretive function.

Our approach also stresses the importance of integrating theory and analysis in a dynamic way (Strauss and Corbin 1990). To facilitate this dynamic relationship, we developed a schema for analysis which took into account technical, textual, playful and collaborative components of the workshop. Our theoretical framework – as outlined earlier – informed these components. In this respect, this study is not only exploratory in terms of trialing *SL* for urban design with high school students but also offers an exploratory approach that contributes to other research using computer-based games or virtual worlds (see Aarseth 1997; Juul 1999). The frameworks developed by these researchers focus on the structural components of games and the rules relating to the game world, characters and objects and their technical or pre-programmed properties. Working from these multiple theoretical and methodological bases, we developed a schema for analysis structured around four topics of interest: technical, textual, playful and collaborative (see Table 1).

Table 1. Schema for analysis and topics of interest.

Technical	Within this category, we consider the elements of the platform – limitations, adjustments and compromises that were necessary to suit the conditions of the workshop. We also address the issue of how much flexibility and freedom of action are possible with the platform, and the degree of choice available to the students.
Textual	Within this category, we consider the narratives that emerged as a spontaneous part of the construction of the textual world of the Lower Mill Site developed in the workshop. Spatial, perspectival and other properties of the virtual world represented are also considered.
Playful	Within this category, we attend to the ways in which 'non-serious' play emerged as a useful learning indicator.
Collaborative	Within this category, we note the observations and reflections that support ways in which collaboration was achieved and limited.

Workshop approach

We reconstructed the Lower Mill Site in its current predevelopment stage on a stand-alone island using the open source 3D application server OpenSimulator. Rather than accessing the commercial version of *SL* (or *Teen SL* [*TSL*]), the dedicated server solution hosting our own island helped us overcome ethical and duty of care concerns in working with underage students. The class was equipped with 20 laptop computers that connected to the OpenSimulator server.

In order to give the students a sense of the spatial and other physical features of the Lower Mill Site, we accompanied them on a half-day excursion to the site. At the site, students were encouraged to explore – the creek, the recently cut-down camphor laurels, the woodworkers' house, the butter factory and the restored mill – to take photographs of things that interested them. A member of the Lower Mill Board and a local councillor briefly addressed the students, telling them a little of the history of the site, the plans for its development and the part they can play in designing a heritage journey at the site.

Following the half-day excursion, we began the workshop with using *Google Earth*™ (GE) to allow the students to explore the area in a more photo-realistic environment. We uploaded a 3D *Google SketchUp*™ (GS) rendering of the proposed library building to illustrate certain qualities of a virtual environment. After an initial training phase to familiarise themselves with the avatar controls that the *SL* client offers, students were asked to brainstorm ideas about both the current and the intended usages of the three main precincts (timber mill, butter factory arts centre and library). Their ideas were recorded on a white board (see Figure 2).

We then focused on the outdoor areas and the greenbelt in the centre of the site, and students were asked to identify ideas and opportunities for how this space could be utilised to enhance the user experience of each of the three precincts – timber mill, butter factory arts centre and library. The class was then divided into three groups representing each one of the three precincts and each group was asked to vote on their favourite idea that was then constructed on the fly in *SL*.

Discussion of results

As we have stated, the primary goal of this study was to undertake an exploratory investigation into the possible advantages of using *SL* as a virtual world platform for engaging students in an urban design project. It is not the intention of this article to provide an in-depth discussion of the formal codes that constitute this particular virtual world medium, nor is it to give 'thick' data description, as the preliminary and short-term nature of the workshop did not enable a more complex process of data collection and analysis. Nevertheless,

Figure 2. Student ideas being constructed on the fly (*Second Life*, Linden Research, Inc., San Francisco, CA, USA).

the workshop yielded rich data, which while narrative in nature, provided insights into the social and learning contexts that the study created. A key purpose is to share our schema and the descriptors we decided upon with a view to prompting further research on the topic. In this section, we have chosen to incorporate the results into our discussion using the categories we established in our schema and by integrating theory and analysis. The four topics of interest outlined in our schema provide a framework around which the discussion of results is structured.

Technical

While our initial intention was to run the workshop within a virtual environment, we also explored other technologies that would assist in presenting the locale relevant to the students and community. Since our plans involved using computers provided by the Apple University Consortium, we focussed our explorations towards software available for the *Mac OSX* operating system. As the following discussion demonstrates, we found that we needed to source alternative platforms and tools at various stages of preparation for the workshop.

Early on in the project, we were supplied with a model of a proposed library for the Lower Mill Site in GS format (Figure 3). GS is a freely available 3D

Figure 3. Screenshot of the Lower Mill Site library model in *Google SketchUp*™ (© 2010 Google).

modelling application, with a simple interface that helps bring 3D modelling to a wider audience. Of particular note to our project are its user-friendly methods for navigating and exploring a 3D world. Students enjoyed zooming in and 'standing' anywhere within a virtual site world in one click, resulting in a 'through your eyes' view. Clicking and dragging the cursor from this position allowed the students to look around their immediate environment. By switching modes (again, one click), the students were able to explore the site by walking in any direction they chose, via the mouse. This intuitive navigation method enabled the students as novice users to quickly learn to control their own explorations of objects in 3D space without needing to memorise multiple mouse and keyboard button combinations, as is the case with similar software.

A useful extension of GS is the ability to upload and view any model created with it within GE, either on a local machine or globally. GE is a freely available application that lets users move around the Earth and zoom in to view terrain, satellite images, buildings and the sea. By uploading the Lower Mill Site library model to GE, we were able to provide an avenue for students to see how its addition would affect the local landscape (Figure 4). Students displayed keen interest in not only exploring the site but also finding their own homes and those of their friends on GE. They also found the control method easy to use and were able to view small details within 3D models. A limitation

Figure 4. The library model was locally embedded in *Google Earth* (© 2009 CNES/ Spot Image; © 2009 MapData Sciences Pty Ltd, PSMA; Image © 2009 Digital Globe; © 2009 Google).

of GE was that it does not include any collision detection on models, so a certain level of immersion is lost when students found themselves walking straight through objects. While GS is better suited towards micro-level exploration, GE was used in the workshop to showcase the library model due to its added flexibility in allowing spatial exploration and comparison at any scale.

We encountered a few crucial issues when considering *SL*. First, minors are not permitted on the main *SL* grid; a special *TSL* world has been set up for this purpose. Setting up an official *TSL* project requires the purchasing of land and background checks on all participants involved, and would require us to work with an external, designated developer. These complications and associated delays were reasons for us to look elsewhere for a solution. Further, importing complex models is a futile task, as essentially, any objects are generally easier to create using the in-world building tools. There are tools available for importing models, such as *AC3D* (http://www.inivis.com/secondlife.html) and Henshin (http://ai-designstudio.net/en/manual/henshinv/what-is-henshin), but *AC3D* proved unsuitable for large complex models such as our library, and Henshin was not an option for our purposes since it requires *AutoCAD* models, which we did not have.

Due to the above restrictions, we turned to open source 3D environments as an alternative solution. The first of these was *RealXtend* (RX) (http://

Figure 5. The library model imported into *RealXtend*.

www.realxtend.org/), at the time, a *Windows*-only virtual world platform that allowed users to set up their own virtual world server, which could serve as a base for building any virtual application. We successfully imported the GS library model into RX using the Ogre Exporter (http://www.di.unito.it/~nunnarif/sketchup_ogre_export/) (Figure 5), which immediately solved one of our problems. However, without access to a fleet of *Windows*-based laptops to use during the workshop at the school, we had to remove RX from our options. The logistics surrounding running RX on 15 Apple laptops (by installing *Microsoft Windows* natively with Bootcamp or virtually via emulation software) were not feasible in the time we had available.

Our eventual solution for a virtual environment platform was *OpenSim* (OS) (http://opensimulator.org/wiki/Main_Page), which offers similar functionality to RX but is available cross-platform. At this point in the project, our focus had shifted from needing to import a pre-existing model to recreating a proposed development site in 3D (Figure 6). With a *Windows* machine set up as the server and properly configured to allow multiple users, the virtual construction of the Lower Mill Site was completed over two days. Our customised chat logger was not functional within OS, but it is likely this had more to do with configuration settings than being a fault of the software itself. In order to connect to our OS server, the *SL* viewer software was installed and launched via the Apple UNIX terminal, with a connection string added which points the *SL* viewer to the IP address of our OS server. Apart from some minor issues with collision detection on the ground plane, OS proved to be stable when running and lag was minimal

Figure 6. A basic replica of the Lower Mill Site in *Second Life* (Linden Research, Inc., San Francisco, CA, USA).

even with 15 laptops accessing the OS server over a virtual private network (VPN) on a shared wireless connection (IEEE 802.11b).

Textual

This first set of workshop activities was aimed at generating various narratives in the form of dialogues between students, and between students, and the planning team and teachers present in the workshop. As the following discussion illustrates, we found that *SL* functioned as a catalyst, providing a dynamic 'boundary object' (Star and Griesemer 1989) to engender and facilitate the development of informed exchanges of ideas, stories and viewpoints.

The Lower Mill Site that had been created on an island in *SL* represented a world that was to some extent already familiar to the students – the vegetation, the butter factory, the mill. It was also a space that opened up the possibility for the students to participate in the production and circulation of narrative. While the students were not asked specifically to construct a story in the *SL* workshop, they inevitably engaged in narratives as they imagined scenarios about the site and its possible development: the people who would visit the 'real' site, the kinds of activities they could engage in and new facilities ('café', 'movie screen', 'graffiti wall', etc.) they could add to the site.

Dividing the class into three groups, each with a designated site brief – the library, the mill, and the butter factory – supported narrative making. Students came up with ideas such as 'shaded outdoor reading areas', 'a graffiti wall', 'outdoor movies', 'a timber-made playground', 'tree lights', 'exhibition displays' and 'a community garden'. These ideas entailed the creation of narratives as students assumed the personae of 'woodies', 'librarians', 'creative artists', 'visitors', 'community members of different ages' and 'local councillors' and explained what they wanted from the site.

The narratives generated in these discussions highlighted several ways for considering how narrative functions almost unnoticed in virtual world platforms such as *SL*. A question that we put to the students was: What can we do in *SL* that we cannot do in the real world? In other words, what are the attributes of *SL* that we can exploit for the purpose of urban design? To replicate activities in *SL* that could be done using 'old' technologies would seem to ignore the qualities that this digital medium offers. By encouraging students to attend to the distinctive attributes of the virtual environment (and available system controls and tools), three elements of the textual world of *SL* emerged from the workshop: perspective, time-space-place and verisimilitude.

Perspective

In the *SL* island of the Lower Mill Site, each student was assigned a female avatar. The server software we used generated a female avatar by default and administration privileges were required to change the gender of the avatar. One of the authors who functioned as both designer and system operator assumed a male avatar. Gendered representation aside, the point is that each student projected themselves as members of the simulated world of the Mill Site by identifying with an assigned avatar. All avatars were numbered, not named (e.g., game user 1). This impersonalised allocation of avatars with students and the students' location outside the virtual world enabled a god-like role for the students who could control the movements of their avatars (Figure 7). The ability to fly, walk, run, flip, spin and change direction (up, down, in circles, etc.) enabled the avatars (and their operators) to navigate the virtual world, alter their perspective and manipulate their own physical perspective as an embodied subject. For example, students could view their avatar from a height, from below or from the side. This shifting perspectival account in relation to 'people' (landscape, objects, etc.) determined the vantage point from which something or someone was represented as being visualised. Such visualisation in the *SL* example enabled phenomena to be focalised by the student/avatar as the perceiving agent. Students therefore assumed an implicit control in that that they were able to shape the textual world and the avatars' movements in that space through a manipulation of perspective.

Time-space-place

Virtual worlds enable movement in 'space', and they must always involve time (Cobley 2001). In the *SL* example, space functioned more as a place that

Figure 7. A group of student avatars meet and chat in-world (*Second Life*, Linden Research, Inc., San Francisco, CA, USA).

was amenable to the design whims of the students. Ryan (2002, 598) sees the purpose of a 'narrative of place' as different from a 'narrative of space' in that the former is intended to 'explore in depth a specific location, to look at all the objects contained in it, and to meet all of its inhabitants'. Apart from not having a community already in place, the *SL* site enabled the students and their avatars to explore the terrain, the established paths and the existing buildings as well as to scrutinise the map of the Lower Mill Site, which appeared at the entrance to the virtual site. While the overarching aim was the design and development of the site, the discussions that evolved as students interacted with the place provided the crucial events along the way to realising this outcome.

Time operated in a dual sense in the workshop. There was a limited amount of time set aside for the workshop, which had to accommodate the normal time schedules of the school day with its 70-minute periods, breaks for morning tea and lunch. There was also the seemingly endless issue of time that permeated the virtual world. While the loss of what Ricoeur (1984–1986) termed 'subjective time' while playing games is regarded by some researchers as a sign of addiction, we consider it as an indicator of their immersion in the workshop activity. We observed that the students focussed on their monitors even while chatting with one another about a problem or asking for assistance. At the end of the session, students found it difficult to finish up. Time also placed demands on both the students and us to ensure that the objectives of the workshop could be achieved. There were also demands on the system operator (Author 4), who was the only person who could construct the design elements the students wanted. As it took time to download tools, build the structure and add design features suggested by the students, he had to work quickly so that all groups could see their ideas materialise on the site. The more flexible aspect of time that operated in the virtual space meant that the passage of time was accelerated: travel could be at high speed, meetings with other avatars could be arranged without delay, buildings could be constructed and demolished within minutes and chats between avatars using the communication function could enable quick exchanges of ideas, greetings or instructions.

Verisimilitude

The final aspect of the textual component of the *SL* site concerns its representation of the world, or more specifically, of the Lower Mill Site. In constructing the virtual world of the site, a process of selecting and articulating some things while leaving other things out was enacted. For example, the proposed library was not included in the site, but a digital model of the library was available for students to view its internal and external dimensions. As explained earlier, for an orientating activity, GE was used to assist the students in locating the site in their local community. In this sense, the *SL* as the example forecloses 'reality' but creates a verisimilitude that is credible, subject to change and revision. While there is a relation between the virtual site and the real site, the notion of verisimilitude offers 'a principle of textual coherence' (Todorov 1977, 87). This notion of textual coherence or verisimilitude is a crucial element for our project as we needed to maintain a general level of credibility which matches as closely as possible with that held by the school, the Lower Mill Board and the Council, who are the partners on our research project. The students' stories about the site – its potential users, possible activities and design features – need to be interpreted by their verisimilitude, their 'truth likeness' or, more accurately, their 'life likeness' (Bruner 1990, 61). Consequently, the stories and design ideas generated in the *SL* workshop are different from other narratives that could be played out in other virtual worlds in that these accounts entail a representation of a community for a purpose. While the purpose behind the workshop involved participation by the students in urban planning, the larger purpose allowed the students to affirm their identities as members of the Lower Mill Site community who have a stake in its future.

Playful

Play emerged as a defining quality of *SL* in the workshop context. The game-like interface was novel and fun for students to explore. They visibly enjoyed flying their avatars through the air, having them leap, run and walk backwards.

An obvious factor behind the learning experience for the students was that there were no winners or losers, which is the usual outcome for a computer game model. However, part of the game appeal was that some choices proved to be unworkable and necessitated an alternative idea. For example, students would find that locating a facility too close to another one created problems with flow of traffic. While *SL* could not be classed as what Ryan (2001, 179) terms a 'text-as-problem category' game, the workshop created the goal or 'problem' for the students to work on. Rather than have students find a correct answer by following textual directions, the 'game' in the workshop had a more metaphorical dimension in that the pleasure for the students appeared to lie in finding a number of possible solutions.

A further playful element was centred on the appearance of their avatars. The design of avatars is a crucial part of the pleasure and identity work that accompanies many digital narratives, especially video games, and, in this case, *SL*. Students quickly wanted to customise their avatars by changing the colour and style of their clothes (or, in some cases, removing the clothes) and hair. Their engagement in the aesthetic modification of the avatars was obviously something they enjoyed doing. It also demonstrated the kind of investment they were prepared to make in the activity and the 'text' as a whole. In other words, the *SL* text engaged them imaginatively, but it could be said that the students became engaged with the text because it demanded something of them. Thus, the investment was intellectual (they had to work out which tools would enable the changes) and productive (they used energy in creating something new). This kind of investment in 'non-serious play' contributed to the characters that inhabited the virtual space; it also produced agency as students actively worked to construct their own version of the avatar that they had been allocated rather than accept what they had been given.

In characterising the students' involvement with *SL* as a game required them to understand it as a rule-governed activity, which was played out for enjoyment as well as for serving a serious purpose. This dual function is a consideration for the kind of constructivist learning we were hoping to encourage. As the workshop was conducted during a school day in a classroom, there were other tacit rules of behaviour operating in the workshop. In one instance, a student was removed from the workshop because a teacher who was observing the activity felt he was misbehaving. A member of the research team explained to the teacher that the workshop was a different kind of activity from the normal school routine and that we wanted the students to experience some freedom. This incident was a testing point for our methodological approach as we wanted the students to see themselves as 'designers' and 'ideas people' working with us in a collaborative, co-learning environment.

The limitations of the platform we were using meant that aspects of the construction of facilities were slow and students had to wait for their turn as the operator responded to their chat messages for particular constructions to be built on a site that they nominated. This waiting time however provided some students with the opportunity to explore the tools that were available to them. One tool they quickly discovered was how to dress and undress an avatar. However, the playful note of naked flying female avatars was silenced when discovered by the teacher. Thus, while there were overt 'rules' operating in the workshop about the task at hand, students also found ways to explore the technology to subvert the tacit rules governing classroom behaviour.

Whereas playing games is often regarded as a pleasurable, non-utilitarian activity, we wanted the workshop to embody the principles of constructivist learning, motivating students to be active in their learning. In an informal discussion with the students a few days after the workshop, they expressed their enthusiasm for the workshop. Many loved the idea of working with a Mac laptop computer and some reported telling their parents about *SL*.

Collaborative

In working with a constructivist approach, our pre-planning of the workshop necessitated finding ways to ensure that the technology would enable the kind of collaborative, active and hands-on involvement that we wanted. We also wanted to engage the mind as well as the hand. Consequently, mindless clicking of a mouse was not a desired function. When exploring GE and GS, we discovered that these tools provided quick and simple avenues for viewing 3D models, but they both lacked a social element and were essentially a single user experience. As we wanted students to be able to communicate and interact with each other while in a 3D space, we decided that these tools would be useful as an orientating activity, but that *SL* would be a good option for communication and interaction.

An early goal for the workshop was to record in-world chat between the students in order to have a record of communications during the exercise. An open source chat logger script was sourced (http://wiki.secondlife.com/wiki/Chat_Logger_(GPL)) and adapted for this purpose, with testing in *SL* providing promising results. With a few simple alterations, we were able to output all chat activity into colour-coded HTML format, ready to be posted to a website and serve as an accurate transcript of user involvement. Another promising open source tool available for *SL* is *Slogbase* (http://slogbase.com/), which creates reports displaying avatar activity over a chosen area (within *SL*) in three dimensions, as well as various statistics on each avatar.

The students responded well to the in-world chat, but as there were more students than laptops (25:15), it meant that students had to take turns or nominate a 'communicator'. Both options worked for ensuring a collaborative mood in the workshop, and the students were good-natured about this restriction. In reviewing the data from the recorded chats, we noted that all the student–student exchanges were mostly social interactions such as greetings, asking about their plans for the weekend, and others were more 'work-related' (drawing attention to features of their avatars, inviting avatars to meet up or comments related to the workshop). Not surprisingly, all the students–system operator exchanges were 'work-related': requests for specific types of buildings to be constructed on specific locations, asking for help, posing questions related to the tools and so on. Thus, the communications function proved important for supporting a range of interactions, scaffolding and active engagement with the technology and the design task.

At several points in the workshop, students required additional information and some of them used the internet or their mobile phones to source this. Jonassen, Peck and Wilson (1999) use the idea of 'manipulation space' to refer to this way of gaining multiple perspectives that enable learners to access different ideas for solving a problem, especially when learners have inadequate prior knowledge.

With three groups devoted to designing ideas to be incorporated into the internal and external spaces of their designated precinct (library, butter factory and mill), the students needed to collaborate within their group to ensure harmony and task completion. They also had to negotiate space claims and conflicting interests. In deciding what to add to their site, students needed to interact with others in their group, agree on one new idea at a time and then decide the best location of the item. For example, the mill group decided to construct a café near their building for visitors, but in deciding the best location, they talked about the need for it to be near the library, as people using the library would also visit the café. They also discussed accessibility to and from the café with respect to the different buildings, and the need for paths, shade, and aesthetic and functional design features. These examples provided a real-world scenario that urban designers face in their professional lives. This need to relate the technology to go beyond non-serious play into a serious mode supports the view that learning with and through technology relates to real-world needs (Forsyth 1993).

The groups' decisions and actions about the location of specific new design items meant that a conceptual point of view comprising all intratextual acts of interpretation was continually made and remade. For example, the students' decisions about design elements were the outcomes of interpretations made in response to inputs by one another. Such interpretations included the kinds of users who would visit the site, events that could be held, actions that other groups had already taken and so on. The students exercised their agency by moving around the virtual world, viewing actions and objects from different points of view and making decisions on design elements. In doing so, they took on various roles as explorers, designers, collaborators and decision-makers within the spatial limits of the *SL* Mill Site.

One final feature of collaboration was in the way students considered the aesthetics of their designs. Just as narrative is a way of knowing, so too is the aesthetic. An aesthetic way of knowing privileges sensory, emotional and affective knowledge. During the half-day excursion to the Lower Mill Site,

Figure 8. Class excursion inspecting the site in real life.

students were encouraged to take digital photographs of textures – tree bark, pebbles, walls and water (Figure 8). These images were then uploaded the next day and used in the workshop to add textual features to the design elements. The process of selecting and photographing an object and then deciding on which one was most suitable for application was part of the aesthetic process and required students to compromise and work as a team in making their decision. The kind of knowledge that the aesthetic brings is important in the design process. Thus, the aesthetic process of the workshop helped to ground the virtual environment in a material reality, whereby there was a corresponding reciprocity between objects in the real world and their translation and application to the virtual world.

Conclusion

The exploratory research reported in this article adds to the growing body of knowledge regarding the use of virtual worlds in learning. By taking urban design as our context, we have also explored ways in which young people can participate actively in a community project. The theoretical and methodological design of our research enabled us to consider how *SL* could be used to engage students in an urban planning workshop and to discern the learning experiences that this medium affords. While the study reported is small scale, it nevertheless provides some positive evidence that *SL* and a constructivist learning approach can provide a useful means for motivating students to be engaged in a real-world learning experience. Characteristics of *SL* that are usually shortcomings for its use in professional urban planning, such as lack of design and positioning precision, were of little or no consequence for the purpose of our workshop trials, but are important considerations if planning to use *SL* for that purpose.

The *SL* workshop took on a flexible learning approach, providing the students with multiple opportunities to engage freely with the technology, to consider the needs of the community and to experience first-hand the Lower Mill Site. Students were immersed in a learning environment while they had a perception of play, through *SL*. Although *SL* is not a game, it has the ability to excite and engage students in a similar way. The use of *SL* opened up opportunities for students that are otherwise unavailable, such as having a significant input into an urban planning project. *SL* provided the additional benefits of students being required to exhibit behaviours such as self-monitoring, problem-solving and decision-making. The students were engaged through *SL* as the carefully constructed learning experiences were scaffolded and complex enough to be challenging.

Collaborative learning was prominent in the workshop and exhibited through the students imagining scenarios about the site and its possible development, in role-playing as various workers at the site and making decisions about design features and site locations, and by having their avatars move around the site, students observed aspects from a different perspective, enabling them to play the role of designers, decision-makers and explorers. By incorporating a real-world experience (excursion to the site), the workshop was able to draw on additional resources such as digital photographs, which proved to be successfully incorporated into the design features. This has implications for considering 'real' textures in urban design instead of relying on computer-generated textures, colours and design elements.

One of the tenets underpinning our approach was respect. After the workshop, students shared their ideas with the architects working on the site and the Lower Mill Board. As one student said: 'It's cool being asked for my ideas. I think they will make my log maze and I have some more ideas for next time'. Students obviously enjoyed having their ideas listened to and being respected by adults. Also, they were excited to be asked to share their work with audiences beyond the classroom and school environment. The Board was impressed with the students' ideas, and one member told the students: 'You have come up with many more ideas than the adult groups who think they know what is best and you did it in less time'. This involvement with the community gave students a way to participate with other local residents and to take ownership of the town's destiny, and in doing so, brought attention to the significance of the role they themselves can play in shaping the future of their hometown.

Acknowledgements

This research is supported under the Australian Research Council's Linkage Projects funding scheme (project number LP0882274). Associate Professor Marcus Foth is the recipient of a Smart Futures Fellowship supported by the Queensland State Government and National ICT Australia. The authors would like to thank our partner organisations: the Regional Council, the local high school and the Lower Mill Site Board, for supporting this research project, as well as Jeremy Hunsinger and the anonymous reviewers for valuable comments on earlier versions of this article. Special thanks to Ross Brown and Rune Rasmussen at QUT, and Andrew Jeffrey at the Apple University Consortium, for their technical support.

References

Aarseth, E. 1997. *Cybertext: Perspectives on ergodic literature.* London: Johns Hopkins University Press.
Barker, C. 2003. *Cultural studies: Theory and practice.* London: Sage.
Bruner, J. 1990. *Acts of meaning.* Cambridge, MA: Harvard University Press.
Buckingham, D. 2000. *After the death of childhood: Growing up in the age of electronic media.* London: Polity.
Cobley, P. 2001. *Narrative.* London: Routledge.
Dede, C. 1995. The evolution of constructivist learning environments: Immersion in distributed, virtual worlds. *Educational Technology* 35, no. 5: 46–52.
Dickey, M.D. 2005. Three-dimensional virtual worlds and distance learning: Two case studies of Active Worlds as a medium for distance learning. *British Journal of Educational Technology* 36, no. 3: 439–51.
Education Queensland. 2005. *Smart classrooms: A strategy for 2005–2007.* http://education.qld.gov.au/smartclassrooms/.
Forsyth, I. 1993. Computers: They'll never replace teachers. In *Proceedings of the 19th ASCILITE Conference*, ed. B. Lo, 253–61. Figtree, New South Wales: Australian Society for Computers in Learning in Tertiary Education (ASCILITE).
Foth, M., B. Bajracharya, R. Brown, and G. Hearn. 2009. The second life of urban planning? Using neogeography tools for community engagement. *Journal of Location Based Services* 3, no. 2: 97–117.
Gordon, E., and G. Koo. 2008. Placeworlds: Using virtual worlds to foster civic engagement. *Space and Culture* 11, no. 3: 204–21.
Huizinga, J. 1955. *Homo Ludens: A study of the play element in culture.* Boston: Beacon Press.
Johnson, L.F., and A.H. Levine. 2008. Virtual worlds: Inherently immersive, highly social learning spaces. *Theory Into Practice* 47: 161–70.
Jonassen, D., K. Peck, and B.G. Wilson. 1999. *Learning with technology: A constructivist perspective.* Upper Saddle River, NJ: Merrill, Prentice-Hall.
Juul, J. 1999. A clash between game and narrative. MA thesis. http://www.jesperjuul.dk/thesis.
Leander, K., and K. McKim. 2003. Tracing the everyday 'sitings' of adolescents on the Internet: A strategic adaptation of ethnography across online and offline spaces. *Education, Communication and Information* 3, no. 2: 211–40.
Pfeil, U., C.S. Ang, and P. Zaphiris. 2009. Issues and challenges of teaching and learning in 3D virtual worlds: Real life case studies. *Educational Media International* 46, no. 3: 223–38.

Ricoeur, P. 1984–1986. *Time and narrative*. 3 vols. Baltimore: Johns Hopkins University Press.

Ryan, M.-L. 2001. *Narrative as virtual reality: Immersion and interactivity in literature and electronic media*. Baltimore: Johns Hopkins University Press.

Ryan, M.-L. 2002. Beyond myth and metaphor: Narrative in digital media. *Poetics Today* 23, no. 4: 581–609.

Sim, S., ed. 2001. *The Routledge companion to postmodernism*. London: Routledge.

Star, S.L., and J.R. Griesemer. 1989. Institutional ecology, 'translations' and boundary objects: Amateurs and professionals in Berkeley's museum of vertebrate zoology, 1907–39. *Social Studies of Science* 19, no. 3: 387–420.

Strauss, A., and J. Corbin. 1990. *Basics of qualitative research: Grounded theory procedures and techniques*. London: Sage.

Todorov, T. 1977. *Théories du symbole*. Paris: Seuil.

Warburton, S. 2009. Second Life in higher education: Assessing the potential for and the barriers to deploying virtual worlds in learning and teaching. *British Journal of Educational Technology* 40, no. 3: 414–26.

The city at play: *Second Life* and the virtual urban planning studio

David Thomas[a] and Justin B. Hollander[b]

[a]*College of Architecture and Planning, University of Colorado, Boulder, Colorado, USA;* [b]*Department of Urban and Environmental Policy and Planning, Tufts University, Medford, Massachusetts, USA*

> This study interrogates the idea of using videogames and game-like virtual worlds as a means to advance studio education pedagogy. Looking at a series of case studies of urban planning courses taught using *Second Life*, the results describe the potentials, and limits, of this emerging digital media. Key findings are that the virtual worlds provided additional benefits to student learning and engagement through fun and intellectual simulation of play. The virtual world environment allowed students to interact in a novel and unique way, improving upon traditional studio education.

For centuries, those who have taught the art and science of planning and designing the physical environment have relied primarily on a studio setting (Lang 1983).[1] These physical studios comprised desks, pencils, pens and, more recently, laptop computers where students work day and night on their projects – in many ways they were the first virtual worlds. The virtual studio today offers a potentially even more profound avenue for teaching urban planning and design within the framework of a videogame.[2] Technological innovations have allowed for the simulataneous participation of an entire class of student planners in a 3D virtual space served on the internet and available nearly anywhere, anytime.

Can the advantages of the design studio in planning education be improved upon by using a videogame?

This article first provides a framework for analyzing the key benefits of the studio setting and the unique challenges of teaching subjects in urban planning and design. Second, a survey of the rationale for using games to teach provides a context for a set of case studies where games were used to teach urban planning and design. These cases describe a set of experimental courses in planning and design that relied heavily on the use of games. Next, we examine the cases in terms of the initial framework, looking how a game-based teaching approach fulfilled the unique learning goals of the planning studio and finally address some of the key challenges to the approach. We conclude by exploring how this new pedagogical strategy for teaching planning may be transferred to other disciplines.

The unique qualities of studio-based learning

City planning was, from its inception, taught primarily through the vehicle of studio-based education (Lang 1983; Heumann and Wetmore 1984). In their study of the history of planning education, Heumann and Wetmore (1984) identified 1909–1970 as a period of growth in the use of studios and workshops, during which time the processes and procedures for students and faculty solidified. These early planning educators saw studios in the same way that architectural educators did, as 'active sites where students are engaged intellectually and socially' (Dutton 1987, 16).

This began to change during the 1970s and 1980s, as planning programs largely began to move away from an emphasis on physical and spatial design toward a social, political, and economic orientation (Heumann and Wetmore 1984; Greene 1988; Pivo 1989; Frank 2006). But in the last 10 years, planning programs have reintroduced studio-based courses. This return to the studio environment can be attributed to the widespread student and faculty interest in physical planning and design. This interest was also, in many ways, a recognition of the robust evidence that studio-based courses are a unique and valuable component in planning education. The literature on studio education suggests five key benefits for student learning in a studio environment over lectures or seminars:

(1) integration and synthesis of knowledge and skills (Schon 1984; Dutton 1987; Greene 1988);
(2) development of teamwork skills (Greene 1988);
(3) application of planning procedures to field example (Heumann and Wetmore 1984);
(4) improvement of problem finding and problem-solving skills (Heumann and Wetmore 1984; Greene 1988); and
(5) provision of a 'professional socializing experience' (Heumann and Wetmore 1984, 124).

Schon (1984) wrote that studios in the visual arts and in architecture are places where 'students learn to make or perform' (2). He noted that in studios, 'everything revolves around the acquisition of artistry through practice and coaching' (2). This intimacy between the teacher and the student allows for an unusually potent 'communicative process of telling and listening, [and] demonstrating and initiating' (9).

There is a growing body of literature in the architecture community about how to apply these studio benefits in a computer environment, what is called 'the virtual design studio' (McCullough, Mitchell, and Purcell 1990). Computer-aided design is the technology at the heart of this virtual studio, but with the advent of massively multiplayer videogames and game-like worlds, the virtual studio has taken on an entirely new definition. These online games are, in many ways, platforms for social networking, playing, and working. With millions of players participating in synthetic online worlds ranging from the fantasy setting of *World of Warcraft* to the open-ended, user-controlled universe of *Second Life*, digital life in the digital age has escaped the pages of science fiction and now appears as a viable platform for education (Bainbridge 2007; Kelton 2007). This article examines the question of whether videogames and game-like online environments can provide additional benefits to the design education studio outlined above.

The role of computer games in planning education

The idea of using games for serious purposes is as old as civilization itself. People have played for the entirety of recorded history and the urge to play remains one of the fundamental signs of intelligent life (Huizinga 1955). People play and through play they learn. The rise of digital technology brought with it a wide variety of opportunities to stimulate learning and evolve pedagogy. Naturally, videogames have attracted attention as a tool for teaching. Placing the subject of videogames in the classroom inside the broader milieu of using computers to teach can appropriately frame digital games in the context of teaching with any new technology (Dumbleton and Kirriemuir 2006).

In an effort to better define and defend the notion of using videogames to teach, advocates of the approach have gathered under the broad banner of 'Serious Games' (Gudmundsen 2006). This movement underlines the interest in using videogames, often commercial games and game development platforms, to achieve more serious, or educational ends. Serious Game developers seek to capture the fun of games and use that to achieve important social or educational ends. The establishment of the Serious Games Initiative by the Woodrow Wilson International Center for Scholars in 2002 and significant investments in the idea, such as the John D. and Catherine T. MacArthur Foundation's 2007 announcement of a $2 million competition around videogames and learning, highlight the growing interest in the subject (MacArthur Foundation 2007).

Meanwhile, scholars of teaching and learning have discovered fresh new territory at the junction of games and pedagogy. Gee (2003) leads a growing body of researchers who see contemporary videogames as providing an important component in a twenty-first-century education. He argues videogames of all types work as learning systems by helping players master different domains of knowledge in a process of situated cognition. Further, because a videogame's success in the market depends on players enjoying the game, game designers inevitably achieve a high level of learning transfer. If gamers cannot play the games, the games do not succeed. Good games, then, are good at teaching (Gee 2005). His research supports the claim made by the Serious Games community that approaches to learning embedded in commercial videogames work equally well to teach gamers or students.

For Gee, the desire to use games to teach initially stems from an interest in sugarcoating less interesting educational content with a candy shell of entertainment. However, this impulse gives way to more significant uses focused on the simulation capabilities of games to put players/learners in a position where they can have experiences in a consequence-free environment.

Or, as Gee states, not only summarizing his interest in the educational possibilities of games but also focusing attention on the source of that potential itself:

> Good video games reverse a lot of our cherished beliefs. They show that pleasure and emotional involvement are central to thinking and learning. (Gee 2007, 2)

Bogost (2006) offers a parallel claim arguing for a notion of 'procedural rhetorics' embedded in games. Game systems mount arguments in terms of their rules and player interactions that may be used in the service of political rhetorics, advertising, and learning. In this way, the game systems themselves, in addition to or in spite of their content, can carry powerful persuasive or educational content. This connection of content to action provides learning through games with a unique educational potential, and one that has been shown to improve the quality of the learning outcomes (Begg, Dewhurst, and Macleod 2005).

The success of using games in education, however, continues to depend on careful design of the learning experiences themselves (Galarneau 2005). Shaffer's (2005) notion of 'epistemic games' clarifies this warning by explaining how motivation and learning rise when students encounter 'thickly authentic' environments that align the interests of the learner with a community of practice's 'ways of doing, being, caring, and knowing.' Epistemic games provide game-like simulations designed to immerse students in professional experiences that mirror actual practice. The outcome can produce better motivated, better educated students.

Using the example of *Madison 2200*, Shaffer describes how students were immersed in an urban design exercise that put them to work redesigning a commercial corridor in Madison, Wisconsin. The outcome of this experience was a rapid immersion in the practice of planning that challenged the participants to think 'like planners' and to enjoy the work in the process.

An interest in moving part of the planning curriculum into the game space follows a similar logic, looking to connect to deeper themes in the human desire to play, using games as a means to interest students in topics that often appear dry or dull, and to simply take advantage of the simulation properties these games possess to enrich static educational content delivery.

This is not new news, even to the field of environmental design.

During the mid-1960s, an interest in the emerging science of 'cybernetics' fueled The Model Cities, a program that sought to increase community participation in urban renewal issues through engagement in games. Driven by federal mandates and funding, community planning education encountered a variety of games, including Francis Hendricks POGE (Planning Operational Gaming Experiment), Allan Feldt's CLUG (Cornell Land Use Game), and others (as described in Light 2008). The use of games in a more professional practice context continues to this day (Steins 2007; Hennessy 2009).

Sanoff's (1979) 'Design Games' remains an influential work on using games as a part of design education, while Wilson (1975) produced an entire series of games to teach patterns of human settlement.

SimCity stands out as a more contemporary example of software, although produced as a game that has been used widely to help teach physical planning and urban design for the past 20 years. Debate over the appropriateness of using *SimCity* as an urban simulator or a teaching tool aside, the idea of using a commercially available videogame inside the planning curriculum is not new (Lobo 2004). Now the advent of sophisticated videogames and virtual world technology opens up design games to the almost infinite possibilities of the digital realm (Simpson 2001). Whether or not games have the potential to dramatically alter the shape of the planning education, the desire to seek new pedagogies and tools in the planning curriculum mirrors ongoing concerns about changes in the planning profession, planning education, and need for curricular reform to keep pace (Carter 1993; Feldman 1994; Friedmann 1994; Guzzetta and Bollens 2003). In this article, we ask how the benefits of learning in a design studio can be met by using the massively multiplayer online virtual world *Second Life*.

Case study: teaching planning using virtual worlds

Over the course of the 2006–2007 academic year, the authors taught six classes in physical planning and design where *Second Life* was used.[3] *Second Life* is a multi-user, 3D virtual environment. It combines game-like qualities inside an open world where the users/players build the landscapes, the buildings, all environmental objects and control the appearance of their in-world personifications, or avatars.

With a history of using games to teach urban planning concepts, the interest in using newer software and gaming platforms to teach was a natural step to take inside a planning department. The selection of *Second Life* was not only based, in part, on its spatial design possibilities but also on its game-like qualities. It looked like fun. While there is considerable debate about the best definition of a game (Juul 2005), and efforts continue to create taxonomies interrelating games, simulations, and virtual worlds (Aldrich 2009), this distinction has never been important in terms of planning education. Playing with urban planning and having fun while exploring urban issues drives the interest in games, game-like environments, and playful simulations.

Second Life, then, was approached as an active sandbox, a playground for learning about planning. And while the structural characteristics of *Second*

Life as a virtual world surely remain important to some forms of analysis, in terms of teaching planning, the world was seen more as a game in the sense described by Galloway as 'an activity defined by rules in which players try to reach some sort of goal' (2006, 19). With the notion of fun, or play, defining the students as players and the educational outcomes structuring the rules and goals, *Second Life* worked as a game world in which to enact specific planning activities.

Of the six courses taught, one was open to both undergraduate and graduate students in graduate programs accredited by the Planning Accreditation Board, and the other five classes were offered as electives in an undergraduate program in environmental studies under the auspices of the Planning Department. While the classes used *Second Life* in different ways, they each required students to utilize the program as a virtual design studio, in a manner as described by McCullough, Mitchell and Purcell (1990).

One of the authors taught the course 'Physical Planning and Design' in the spring of 2007. Another author taught the course 'Planning in the Gaming World: Urban Planning Concepts Using Games and Virtual Worlds' from the spring of 2006 to the fall of 2008.

In all six courses, the instructors introduced the *Second Life* program early in the semester and the program was used both inside and outside class time through the semester. In one course, students were tasked with developing a site development plan for roughly 10 acres of vacant land adjacent to a mass transit station in a local neighborhood. In another class, students were assigned several projects where they experimented with land use conflict by building places in *Second Life* focused on the themes of 'learning,' 'relaxation,' and 'having fun.'

As instructors, we took time to study *Second Life* before developing our courses. One of the authors' first experiences was erecting a simple rectangular structure, planting some grass and a few trees. A few days later, he returned to find the simple structure overrun with hundreds of additional trees, strange glowing watermelons, and an ominous-looking attack helicopter hovering above the little plot of land. He soon encountered another in-world character or avatar and quickly learned that the visiting avatar was a teaching assistant for an architectural design class at the University of Westminster (UK). His job was to help students in his class with subdividing property, grading land, and assisting students with modeling. He was a virtual teaching assistant. He explained that other 'residents' of *Second Life* had seen the class' parcel of land and decided to have fun, planting fruit and war weaponry. With a few keystrokes, the instructor was able to remove all the unwanted objects from the parcel. With all the other objects out of the way, he noticed that the grass and trees that he had planted just days prior were still overgrown and required maintenance. Even before the students were plugged in, we as instructors learned a lot in this new universe very quickly.

For the students, their first exposure to *Second Life* was universally positive in all six classes. Students took time to conceive their own virtual identity and created avatars.[4] In this allotted time of experimentation, some students in one class wandered off the island designated for the class project and began cavorting with others. Here, one student met students at a nearby parcel who were at a European university. They invited him to join a satanic cult saying, 'come over to the dark side.' He successfully resisted and joked to the rest of the class about it.

Peter Filene (2005) writes in *Joy of teaching* about the importance of providing 'diversions' in the classroom, particularly the need to offer visual stimulation. Rather than just showing a slide of a neighborhood in Amsterdam to make a point, *Second Life* allowed us to, as a class, walk the streets of the neighborhood.[5] It helped us as teachers do our job in the same way that a field trip can help. It offered a social/communal experience where students could experience places in their own way.

Students in one course had little prior experience in 3D modeling and were largely intimidated by the difficulty of creating objects in *Second Life*. Students in another class had, on average, considerable experience in 3D but they, too, were quite frustrated with *Second Life* because of its unique proprietary modeling system, which they found limited and awkward compared to more familiar tools.[6] Equally surprising was the general disinterest by most students in using *Second Life* for personal, non-academic use. Given that the students were all, by definition, part of the internet generation, we assumed they would start joining social groups and 'hanging out' with friends online. They did not. They largely felt that *Second Life* was not that interesting and they were busy with their other classes and extra-curricular activities. While many our students shied away from the social dimensions of *Second Life*, clearly there is interest with a membership in this virtual world of over nine million (at the time of writing).

Through an iterative process, the students created, walked through, experienced, flew-over, and re-conceived their plans. As hoped for, the students had a genuine collaborative experience in *Second Life*. One student said, 'last night, Jane and Alfred and I were all on *Second Life* working on the project. It was really cool, we showed each other what we were doing, made suggestions to each other.'

While generally skeptical about the building tools available in the world, the students in one course expressed a consistent positive response to a fully online class meeting. Having the entire class log in from remote locations, meeting at a specified in-world location, receiving and discussing an assignment was seen as a success. The convenience of attending class from their own location coupled with the direct and terse interaction provided by *Second Life*'s text chat system worked to deliver something unlike a classroom experience. This contributed to the student perception of *Second Life* as a unique place. At the very least, the online meeting was seen pragmatically. 'At least we didn't have to come to class that day,' stated several students.

The biggest challenge faced in teaching with *Second Life* was confronting the fact that this 'virtual' world was real in many ways. On a few occasions, students and staff involved in both classes were harassed by other avatars. Vandalism was a problem on a number of occasions. And the whole *Second Life* universe has an overtly sexual tone. One student remarked, 'There's a command on the Edit menu that says "take off clothing" – that's really weird.'[7]

In one of the classes, students were warned that as an active, living world they might encounter objectionable or offensive content. Further, the instructor emphasized that the instances of social disturbance and interference common to *Second Life* reflected the conflicting interests and antagonistic behavior that remains one of the key challenges to planning in the real world. Learning to negotiate and manage a diverse social environment was one of the course objectives and *Second Life* provided a perfect laboratory for understanding the planning process as something much more than theoretical design and management.

Examples of student work from one class are presented in Figures 1 and 2. Overall, the students were able to successfully master the basic building tools

Figure 1. Looking south, this is an aerial view of the linear park, community center, and affordable housing the students in the Tufts class designed for the Forest Hills neighborhood (*Second Life*, Linden Research, Inc., San Francisco, CA, USA).

Figure 2. Looking north, with the City of Boston in the background, this image shows a new mixed-use retail and artist space on the left and existing housing on the right (*Second Life*, Linden Research, Inc., San Francisco, CA, USA).

of *Second Life* and use it in their planning and design education. Students in both courses were able to integrate planning concepts and tools when completing their *Second Life* assignments, despite technological constraints in the *Second Life* software made the construction of land use plans and maps difficult and the resulting student work reflects that limitation. In the class with students experienced in other 3D building tools, student frustration with the *Second Life* tools led one of the authors to eliminate the structural quality as an assessment criterion and instead focus on student descriptions and critical assessment of their building concepts. In the course with students less experienced with 3D building, their work was assessed generously as they were piloting new software.

Interestingly, while the novelty of executing plans in *Second Life* was part of what made the class fun, it also worked somewhat as an impediment to students' full engaging in the idea that they were working on 'real' planning activities. A typical student comment on the assignments would state, 'Unlike designing in the real world where one must consider a full site analysis and all the variables surrounding the site, we just of just went for it – largely because you can in *Second Life*.'

Results and discussion

Observations about the apparent efficacy of using a game environment such as *Second Life* provide a framework for future research. As the popularity of videogames continues to grow and movements such as Serious Games provide an encouraging context for learning with games, more attention is needed around specific pedagogies, approaches, and methods for moving beyond the excitement of working with something new, and maximizing the educational potential of this emerging medium. In this sense, the cases provided in this study provide part of a rationale for further inquiry into the subject of teaching urban planning through games, without providing a clear picture into the long-term value of such an approach.

Of particular note is the timeline during which these classes occurred. *Second Life* was a relatively new virtual world platform and was just beginning to attract attention inside higher education. As such, these courses were among the first to offer urban planning curriculum in the virtual world. Since these courses were offered, the idea of using *Second Life* inside the planning curriculum, and in the professional planning world, has grown.

So, in a sense, the results of this inquiry should be framed inside an era of *Second Life* that predates many of the accomplishments and pedagogical insights that were to come. As such, while preliminary, the results of this study provide a particular insight into dealing with education on an emerging platform, rather than a particular view of gaming as an emerging educational practice.

Looking back at the history of using games to teach planning students, and to engage communities in planning activities, we can see that improving our models for using games continues to drive an interest in research.

Consider the situation of *SimCity*, a game used both as a part of the planning curriculum and otherwise influential on the discipline (Lobo 2004). Yet after 20 years of influence, only recently has the subject of using *SimCity* to teach inside the planning curriculum been directly addressed in the planning literature (Gaber 2007). It seems wise to approach potential curriculum innovations in a timelier manner.

In this context, since the current analysis of teaching planning using online games relies on the experience of the authors in prototype courses using the game environment *Second Life* and their explorations of the potential of games as a teaching medium, the results are likewise preliminary.

In returning to the original five key benefits of a traditional studio experience, we present Table 1 where we summarize how well the *Second Life* experience met each benefit. This summary is a result of an informal comparison of instructor experiences across the courses in the case study and is supported by specific feedback gathered by both instructors during the delivery of the courses.

Second Life appeared to improve students' integration of knowledge and skills and teamwork skills, had no impact on their application of planning

Table 1. Comparison of key benefits of a traditional design studio with the *Second Life* experience.

Key benefits of traditional studio	Experience using *Second Life*
Integration and synthesis of knowledge and skills	*Second Life improved this benefit.* We introduced 3D models of actual places in *Second Life* for them to use as a site for integrating their knowledge and skills. Further, building inside a synthetic social space also emphasized the complexities of executing planning efforts in the real world, understanding contest and conflict in use as well as the complexities of negotiating with various interests.
Development of teamwork skills	*Second Life improved this benefit.* Teamwork in the twenty-first century works across space and time and *Second Life* facilitated student collaboration and teamwork at all hours of the day and night.
Application of planning procedures to field example	*Second Life had no impact on this benefit.* Students were generally able to apply planning procedures to field examples but the benefits of working within a virtual world had no bearing on student learning in this area.
Improvement of problem finding and problem-solving skills	*Second Life had some impact on this benefit.* Students were able to successfully improve their problem finding and problem solving skills. The use of 'authentic experiences' provided by the virtual world improved the depth and range of student learning in this area.
Provision of a 'professional socializing experience'	*Second Life had no impact on this benefit.* While students chose not to utilize the social networking features of the program, they did interact socially with one another.

procedures to field examples, had some impact on their problem finding/solving skills, and did not impact on their professional socializing experiences. Based on these results, we feel that the best classroom format embraces *Second Life*, embraces some purely online class meetings, and also embraces the traditional classroom environment. This hybrid learning environment appears to offer the most opportunities for students to learn in ways they are comfortable with and to allow opportunities for the critical face-to-face socializing elements of the conventional studio and reflects recent evidence that hybrid online/classroom courses result in the best adherence to learning outcomes, when compared to strictly online or classroom experiences (U.S. Department of Education 2009). Our experience was that as long as students were afforded some in-class socializing time, they were able to enjoy online most of the benefits of the traditional studio outlined in the literature.

On a less formal note, both instructors believe that by framing more traditional educational practices inside the fun context of a game holds much promise. While dealing with stormtroopers and dragons inside a planning context might reduce the feeling of authentic practice, these elements do model the somewhat contentious, surprising, and uncontrollable factors that planners encounter in the real world. In this view, the unpredictable elements that make a world like *Second Life* fun also model one of the most difficult aspects of the planning curriculum: teaching students about the variable nature of people and their desires in terms of the built environment.

Further, we believe that while general pedagogical principles can be applied to games (or game principles to general education), special attention must be paid to the specifics of the subject matter at hand. For example, design students often struggle with the nature of cities: Are they constructed using timeless principles and scientifically rigorous formulas, or do they emerge from a messy process of human contest? The answer, as any practitioner can tell you, is both. Finding games and game-like simulations that bring these two tendencies into focus is a specialized challenge for the planning educator. And, as this study suggests, software such as *Second Life* provides an almost ideal combination of both characteristics.

As planning educators, we often confront how technology changes the metropolis and professional practice. In this article, we hoped to help readers consider how the emergence of videogames and game-like worlds may change the way we teach physical planning.

In considering the conclusions drawn, it is important to note the limitations of this work and of the use of *Second Life* in the classroom. This study focuses on the use of *Second Life* in six courses across a handful of academic years[8] and, as such, does not propose to represent a longitutinal study of learning effects or even a comprehensive catalog of teaching techniques of use to the planniner educator.

During the time period these courses were taught, *Second Life* presented important technological drawbacks. The system's proprietary prims method of design was completely incompatible with other 3D design applications. As a result, if a designer created an object (i.e., the White House) in another 3D software program, she was unable to then import that object into *Second Life*. All designing must occur within the application and this led to frustration on the part of students. Of course, software engineers may overcome these challenges and find ways to ease the conversion of objects from one application to another.

Conversely, the conventional tools for planning and designing the physical environment include *AutoCAD* and *SketchUp*. Those programs help students refine their skills and develop technique, but have no connection with any tangible places or people. Such programs pale in comparison with what

Second Life offers: it creates a forum to explore planning and design as social interactions and processes, rather than as simply knowledge and technique. *Second Life* introduces an element of the real world in real time that can be a powerful learning agent; it does not come without problems.

The most ironic part of the virtual studio is that it is, in many senses, quite real. In our classes, students' work was vandalized, they were harassed, and they were made to feel uncomfortable by overt sexuality. In other *Second Life* locations, worse has happened. *The Chronicle of Higher Education* has run several news stories in the last year of harassment and threatening behavior in *Second Life* (Foster 2007a, 2007b). These incidents led one columnist to suggest that *Second Life* was just too dangerous for professors and recommended greater prudence in using it for college learning (Bugela 2007).

The fact that a game can be considered to be too dangerous may be further evidence that student experiences and more importantly their learning that occurs in the *Second Life* environment is very real. In Shaffer's term, *Second Life can become* 'thickly authentic' to the planning student.

Conclusion

As digital technology transforms all forms of knowledge work, including the environmental design disciplines, it is clear that virtual worlds, such as *Second Life*, provide a context and model for the future of design. Allowing students to coordinate design and building activities while separated in both time and space offers tantalizing possibilities for the future of design. Design reviews and community participation in design take on new possibilities when one considers the relatively low barriers to entry. In most cases, a personal computer and a network connection is all that someone needs to join in the review and revision of design proposals.

As one of the authors has argued elsewhere, the critical issue when using new technology such as videogames to teach is not whether or not students can use them to learn, but what exactly students learn (Thomas 2005). The current survey of efforts to teach in *Second Life* shows a promising, but mixed bag of success at achieving established goals for planning education.

Along those lines, some key questions still need to be answered:

- Are students learning a new, multimodal form of communication necessary to succeed in a wired, global economy?
- How is communication of design and intent either adapted to or changed by the introduction of 3D multi-participant technology? Assuming all or most students have played videogames prior to entering these environments, how are the perception of the virtual classroom and the accompanying learning objectives changed by previous notions games and what makes them fun?

- Is teaching in an online world a better investment of limited resources over more traditional face-to-face studios?

As educators, we can only state that we have a lot of playing left to do!

Notes

1. This is a fully extended and reworked version of an earlier short commentary article published as Hollander, J.B., and D. Thomas. 2009. Virtual planning: 'Second Life' and the online studio. *Journal of Planning Education and Research* 29, no. 1: 108–13.
2. This article uses the general term 'videogame' to describe any interactive electronic entertainment, including computer games.
3. All the classes were taught in a studio/face-to-face lab environment. However, one course met virtually for one week, where students only met inside *Second Life*, from remote locations.
4. Avatars are the virtual representation of a user in *Second Life*, 'The character a player controls in a game, or the personification of the player in a game's world' *Videogame style guide and reference manual* (2007).
5. Not all cities' neighborhoods have been virtually modeled in *Second Life*, but the numbers are growing quickly.
6. The *Second Life* modeling system is based on a molar framework where each object comprises prims. These prims are the building blocks for everything in *Second Life*. Other 3D modeling software programs utilize vectors and planes to construct objects – the two systems are not generally interchangeable and at this point, *Second Life* does not support importing of any geometries created in tools outside of the game world.
7. Because *Second Life* avatars are fully customizable, there are cases where removing all costuming and clothing is desirable.
8. Planning in the Gaming World has been offered a total of five semesters through the fall of 2007.

References

Aldrich, C. 2009. Virtual worlds, simulations, and games for education: A unifying view. *Innovate: Journal of Online Education* 5, no. 5.

Bainbridge, W.S. 2007. The scientific research potential of virtual worlds. *Science* July 31: 472–6.

Begg, M., D. Dewhurst, and H. Macleod. 2005. Game-informed learning: Applying computer game processes to higher education. *Innovate: Journal of Online Education* 1, no. 6.

Bogost, I. 2006. *Unit operations: An approach to videogame criticism.* Cambridge, MA: MIT Press.

Bugela, M.J. 2007. Second thoughts on *Second Life. The Chronicle of Higher Education*, September 21.

Carter, E.J., Jr. 1993. Toward a core body of knowledge: A new curriculum for city and regional planners. *Journal of Planning Education and Research* 12, no. 1: 160–3.

Dumbleton, T., and J. Kirriemuir. 2006. Digital games and education. In *Understanding digital games*, ed. J. Rutter and J. Bryce, 223–40. London/Thousand Oaks, CA: Sage.

Dutton, T.A. 1987. Design and studio pedagogy. *Journal of Architectural Education* 41, no. 1: 16–25.

Feldman, M.M.A. 1994. Perloff revisited: Reassessing planning education in post-modern times. *Journal of Planning Education and Research* 13, no. 2: 89–103.

Filene, P. 2005. *The joy of teaching: A practical guide for new college instructors.* Chapel Hill: University of North Carolina Press.

Foster, A.L. 2007a. Virtual worlds as social-science labs: How one professor uses online games as Petri dishes of human behavior. *The Chronicle of Higher Education*, July 6.

Foster, A.L. 2007b. The death of a virtual campus. *The Chronicle of Higher Education*, July 13.

Frank, A.I. 2006. Three decades of thought on planning education. CPL Bibliography 376. *Journal of Planning Literature* 21, no. 1: 15–67.

Friedmann, J. 1994. Planning education for the late twentieth century: An initial inquiry. *Journal of Planning Education and Research* 14, no. 10: 55–64.

Gaber, J. 2007. Simulating planning: SimCity as a pedagogical tool. *Journal of Planning Education and Research* 27, no. 2: 113–21.

Galarneau, L. 2005. Authentic learning experiences through play: Games, simulations and the construction of knowledge. Paper presented at the DiGRA 2005 Conference: Changing Views – Worlds in Play, June, in Vancouver.

Galloway, A.R. 2006. *Gaming: Essays on algorithmic culture, electronic mediations.* Minneapolis: University of Minnesota Press.

Gee, J.P. 2003. *What video games have to teach us about learning and literacy.* 1st ed. New York: Palgrave Macmillan.

Gee, J.P. 2005. What would a state of the art instructional video game look like? *Innovate: Journal of Online Education* 1, no. 6.

Gee, J.P. 2007. *Good video games + good learning: Collected essays on video games, learning, and literacy.* New York: P. Lang.

Greene, S. 1988. Making the studio experience work for part-time students. *Journal of Planning Education and Research* 8, no. 1: 9–11.

Gudmundsen, J. 2006. Movement aims to get serious about games. *USA Today*, May 19.

Guzzetta, J.D., and S.A. Bollens. 2003. Urban planners' skills and competencies: Are we different from other professions? Does context matter? Do we evolve? *Journal of Planning Education and Research* 23, no. 1: 96–106.

Hennessy, C. 2009. Professor leads team that won MacArthur foundation grant. *Emmerson College Today*, May 2009.

Heumann, L.F., and L.B. Wetmore. 1984. A partial history of planning workshops: The experience of ten schools from 1955 to 1984. *Journal of Planning Education and Research* 4, no. 2: 120–30.

Huizinga, J. 1955. *Homo ludens: A study of the play-element in culture.* Boston: Beacon Press.

Juul, J. 2005. *Half-real: Video games between real rules and fictional worlds.* Cambridge, MA: MIT Press.

Kelton, A.J. 2007. *Second Life: Reaching into the virtual world for real-world learning* (Research Bulletin). Boulder, CO: EDUCAUSE Center for Applied Research.

Lang, J. 1983. Teaching planning to city planning students: An argument for the studio/workshop approach. *Journal of Planning Education and Research* 2, no. 2: 122–9.

Light, J. 2008. Taking games seriously. *Technology and Culture* 48: 28.

Lobo, D.G. 2004. Playing with urban life: How *SimCity* influences planning culture. *The Next American City*, Issue 6.

MacArthur Foundation. 2007. *MacArthur announces $2 million new digital media and learning competition.* http://www.macfound.org/site/c.lkLXJ8MQKrH/b.1053853/apps/nl/content2.asp?content_id={CB00292A-1602-403E-9FE9-5F392B5274F4}&notoc=1.

McCullough, M., W.J. Mitchell, and P. Purcell, eds. 1990. *The electronic design studio: Architectural knowledge and media in the computer era.* Cambridge, MA: MIT Press.

Pivo, G. 1989. Specializations, faculty interest, and courses in physical planning subjects at graduate planning schools. *Journal of Planning Education and Research* 9, no. 1: 19–27.

Sanoff, H. 1979. *Design games.* Experimental ed. Los Altos, CA: W. Kaufmann.

Schon, D.A. 1984. The architectural studio as an exemplar of education for reflection-in-action. *Journal of Architectural Education* 38, no. 1: 2–9.

Shaffer, D.W. 2005. Epistemic games. *Innovate: Journal of Online Education* 1, no. 6.

Simpson, D.M. 2001. Virtual reality and urban simulation in planning: A literature review and topical bibliography. *Journal of Planning Literature* 15, no. 3: 359–76.

Steins, C. 2007. A parallel universe: What the virtual world can do for planning. *Planning* 73, no. 1: 16–20.

Thomas, D. 2005. Messages and mediums: Learning to teach with videogames. *On the Horizon* 13, no. 2: 89–94.

U.S. Department of Education. 2009. *Office of planning, evaluation, and policy development, evaluation of evidence-based practices in online learning: A meta-analysis and review of online learning studies.* Washington, DC: U.S. Department of Education.

Wilson, F. 1975. *City planning: The games of human settlement.* New York: Van Nostrand Reinhold.

The potential for scientific collaboration in virtual ecosystems

Brian Magerko

School of Literature, Communication and Culture, Georgia Institute of Technology, Atlanta, Georgia, USA

This article explores the potential benefits of creating *virtual ecosystems* from real-world data. These ecosystems are intended to be realistic virtual representations of environments that may be costly or difficult to access in person. They can be constructed as 3D worlds rendered from stereo video data, augmented with scientific data, and then deployed online for use. The application of virtual ecosystems stretches from interdisciplinary scientific research that may not occur otherwise to providing science students with an environment to conduct studies and virtual field trips in that they would otherwise not have access to.

Introduction

There are significant meta-level issues in scientific research that have beset scientists since the founding of their fields. It is common to find in specializations of scientific fields that information sharing and collaboration decreases as fields specialize. For example, it is unlikely that artificial intelligence researchers are aware of the work that their colleagues in VLSI design are doing, despite being in the same broad field of electrical engineering and computer science. More significantly, scientists often depend on expensive equipment (e.g., using a particle collider) or costly site visits (e.g., visiting a remote Pacific island) to conduct their research. These problems exist at the cost of potential collaborations and discoveries that could be made by individuals within and across scientific disciplines.

Virtual environments (VEs) have the potential for addressing the issues described above. VEs have been explored as tools for conducting ethnographic research, economics studies, and scientific experiments with virtual equipment (Bainbridge 2007). VEs have several features that make them enticing for such academic work. First, VEs are relatively *inexpensive*. Once the time and work has been put into building an environment, only maintenance work need be put in. Contrast this cost to the ongoing funds put into individual researchers or labs funding their own excursions or equipment, and the savings in cost (for our society) over time become evident. Second, VEs that provide tools for users to *contribute* their own content (e.g., *Second Life* users can build their own persistent objects in the world) can add content without significant cost to developers. Third, VEs provide a medium that allows for the significant presentation of scientific data *in situ*. As opposed to presenting content in decontextualized forms (e.g., in spreadsheets), scientists can use VEs to directly associate the presentation of data with the phenomenon they are studying. The field of scientific visualization exists to explore the potential of representing data in a visual, and often contextualized, form (McCormick, DeFanti, and Brown 1988).

Our observation that VEs can be used to visualize scientific data *in situ* leads us to consider that there are specific fields, such as environmental or ocean sciences, where they visually observe and collect data from real 3D environments, such as coral reef systems, wetlands, or forests. We hypothesize that VEs are an appropriate fit for the aforementioned research meta-level issues within the field of environmental sciences. The development of *virtual ecosystems* (VEs that represent real ecosystems) for scientific discovery and collaboration has the potential to create powerful research tools for environmental scientists that both mitigate the high cost of field work and encourage interdisciplinary work in related fields that are otherwise disparate.

Virtual ecosystems

Virtual ecosystems that are created from real-world data to represent an actual reality-based ecosystem present a powerful application for scientific research within virtual worlds. While other research studies human behavior in existing VEs, the creation of virtual ecosystems allows researchers (or students) to study the environment itself. Scientists can therefore visually and spatially examine a space of interest without the cost of transporting themselves and their equipment to that space.

The question of how to build a digital copy of a real environment is a major issue with the creation of virtual ecosystems. 3D artists could effectively do the work, but that is an incredibly large, expensive, and timely approach. An alternative is to visit the environment, collect data on that environment, and then use that data to automatically (or semi-automatically) reproduce the environment on a computer. Our research group's process of creating a virtual ecosystem based on real-world 3D data involves processing the captured data using a class of algorithms to build a 3D geometric model called *Structure from Motion* or *SFM* (Dellaert et al. 2000; Steedly, Essa, and Dellaert 2003; Ni, Steedly, and Dellaert 2007). These algorithms take either a video sequence or a collection of images and produce a 3D model of the scene. Other approaches, such as image-based rendering and video-rendering methods (Schödl et al. 2000; Schödl and Essa 2002), can be used to then render the data into a usable 3D environment.

Research has shown that the fidelity of a digital experience is not necessarily positively correlated with the desired effects. For example, the *uncanny valley* (e.g., MacDorman 2006) is well known as a point at which the increasing fidelity of a digital character becomes negatively correlated with the believability of that character. 'Very lifelike' might be much more disturbing than a more abstract representation. In terms of VEs, studies have shown that there may be a negative correlation with high-fidelity experiences and learning environments. Mayer (2005) asserts '...people learn more deeply from a multimedia message when extraneous material is excluded rather than included' (184). However, this is unlikely to be an issue with virtual ecosystems since scientists commonly conduct research *in situ* where the fidelity of the experience is higher than we could hope to capture with current technologies.

We are currently creating a virtual coral reef ecosystem based on video data collected at the Andros Barrier Reef. A scuba diver collected data by making crisscross traversals across an area of interest with two high-definition video cameras mounted on a frame. The resulting VE will allow researchers to place their own work, and that of others, into a large-scale ecosystem framework to aid in the interpretation of their results (thus freeing them from an over-dependence on results gathered over a handful of research dives, for example). Furthermore, there are many aspects of reef health that can be studied using only the VE itself, including species diversity, coral colony size, algal cover, degree of bleaching, etc., at scales that are representative of an entire reef system. The VE will provide a way to collate, index, and contextualize a wealth of interdisciplinary scientific data that would be difficult to glean from the scientific literature. For example, a biologist would certainly benefit from temperature logging data collected by a climate scientist some years earlier at her research site. Likewise, the climate scientist might be able to use the biologist's salinity data to look at current patterns on the reef. Many such datasets go unpublished, yet would be perfect candidates for a virtual coral reef laboratory.

Previous work has been done on collaborative virtual environments (CVEs) (e.g., Barab et al. 2005). However, little work has been done on how realistic environments can be used for work that incorporates scientific data as a key element for collaboration and research. We are creating an environment that not only provides features that are common to CVEs, such as *embodiment* (i.e., representations of users as animated avatars), *virtual spaces*, and *group telecommunication*, but also allows group interactions to take place in a realistic virtual ecosystem that contains relevant scientific data that can be visualized and manipulated by researchers.

The visualization of scientific data (e.g., ocean currents, temperature change, acidification, fauna populations, etc.) within a virtual ecosystem has three main purposes. The first is to provide access to relevant local and global data within the space being studied. With the ability to visualize, compare, manipulate, and annotate data within the target ecosystem, scientists will have a powerful tool for online scientific collaboration and experimentation. This would help facilitate online scientific discovery and collaboration in a space that is either remote or no longer in existence. A strong consequence of this approach is that virtual spaces could be used as a portal for scientific data that visualizes spaces that do not exist anymore. The second purpose would be to present data that would be of interest to science students (which is discussed further below), making them aware of the key scientific issues as it relates to natural and human ecosystems. The third is to foster new ways of thinking about complex systems by providing access to both local and global environmental data in a contextualized manner (e.g., of the kind of relationships and data relevant to the health of coral reefs, from everyday human activity to specific health issues that reefs have). We contend that by bringing all of this knowledge to bear within the context of the target environment, scientists and students will be able to directly reason about the relationship between far away effects (e.g., human electricity use) and the health of the ecosystem.

Future work and issues

Once the virtual ecosystem is created, we will evaluate whether we should use currently available 3D game technology or create our own custom application to allow scientists to remotely log in and explore the space with a virtual avatar. Users will be able to contribute their own data in an XML-defined format, browse and select different datasets, and chat with other users online. A key feature will be to visualize data in both a private (only that user can see it) and public (everyone can see it) manner so that scientists can do work on their own while others are online as well as work as a group. However, we will not understand how users should be able to interact with each other and the data within a group setting until we can do an evaluative study of a completed prototype.

An open question regarding the practical use of VEs for scientific research of this nature is related to the buy-in needed from researchers to contribute data. Consistent use of data repositories has had a very mixed history across academic fields; therefore, ease of use and visibility will be crucial to the success of using VEs for the sharing of scientific data. Organizing conferences to be held in the space and requiring a submission of data is one feasible approach to increase the visibility and relevance of an environment. An alternative approach is for the maintainers of a virtual ecosystem to coordinate with research groups to encourage them to share their data, even if only in raw form, for uploading.

The process of data collection is also an additional concern. Whether it is a land-based or marine ecosystem, there is a difficulty in collecting a large amount of data over a space using handheld cameras. Future work will explore the possibility of using multiple robots to swarm over an area, greatly reducing the time cost in data collection.

Aside from applications in scientific collaboration, an accessible, data-rich virtual ecosystem could potentially also be used as an educational tool for higher education science students. For example, Barab et al. (2005) have already begun using virtual cultural heritage sites as platforms for educational computer games. Students could log in to a virtual ecosystem and virtually visit a locale that they would likely never visit on a field trip. Students, with guidance from their teacher, could have access to the same datasets used by scientists and can conduct experiments by manipulating that data. Additional development would need to be done to provide students with the appropriate interface to the environment, tools to operate on the data, etc.; however, the potential application has definite potential. Our future work will focus on developing a more structured, game-based curriculum incorporated into an educational version of the application that students can make use of with or without a teacher's guidance (Magerko, Stensrud, and Holt 2006). As mentioned earlier, there is the question as to whether or not the high-fidelity nature of what is discussed here would have a negative impact on learning. However, the focus of the presentation needs to be on the scientific-related data (e.g., the visualization of the environment and related scientific data), with a subsequent de-emphasis on unrelated features of the learning experience to address the earlier mentioned concerns about the possible negative effect of high-fidelity virtual experiences on learning (e.g., do not worry about making a hyper-realistic model of how to navigate underwater since we are not concerned with teaching about how to scuba dive).

Acknowledgements
Thanks to my collaborators, Dr Kim Cobb, Dr Frank Dellaert, Tanyoung Kim, and Carlos Nieto for their efforts on collecting data at Andros and to the GVU Center at Georgia Tech for funding this work.

References
Bainbridge, W. 2007. The scientific research potential of virtual worlds. *Science* 317: 472–6.
Barab, S.A., M. Thomas, T. Dodge, R. Carteaux, and H. Tuzun. 2005. Making learning fun: Quest Atlantis, a game without guns. *Educational Technology Research and Development* 53, no. 1: 86–108.

Dellaert, F., S.M. Seitz, C.E. Thorpe, and S. Thrun. 2000. Structure from motion without correspondence. Paper presented at the IEEE Computer Society Conference on Computer Vision and Pattern Recognition (CVPR), June, in Carnegie Mellon University, Pittsburgh, PA.

MacDorman, K.F. 2006. Subjective ratings of robot video clips for human likeness, familiarity, and eeriness: An exploration of the uncanny valley. Paper presented at the ICCS/CogSci-2006 Long Symposium: Toward Social Mechanisms of Android Science, July 26, in Vancouver.

Magerko, B., B. Stensrud, and L. Holt. 2006. Bringing the schoolhouse inside the box – A tool for engaging, individualized training. Paper presented at the 25th Army Science Conference, November, in Orlando, FL.

Mayer, R.E. 2005. *The Cambridge handbook of multimedia learning.* New York: Cambridge University Press.

McCormick, B.H., T.A. DeFanti, and M.D. Brown. 1988. Visualization in scientific computing. *ACM SIGBIO Newsletter* 10, no. 1.

Ni, K., D. Steedly, and F. Dellaert. 2007. Out-of-core bundle adjustment for large-scale 3D reconstruction. Paper presented at the IEEE International Conference on Computer Vision (ICCV), October 14–21, in Rio de Janeiro.

Schödl, A., and I. Essa. 2002. Controlled animation of video sprites. Paper presented at the 2002 ACM SIGGRAPH/Eurographics Symposium on Computer Animation, July, in San Antonio, TX.

Schödl, A., R. Szeliski, D.H. Salesin, and I. Essa. 2000. Video textures. In *Proceedings of the 27th Annual Conference on Computer Graphics and Interactive Techniques.* New York: ACM Press/Addison-Wesley.

Steedly, D., I. Essa, and F. Dellaert. 2003. Spectral partitioning for structure from motion. Paper presented at the IEEE International Conference on Computer Vision (ICCV), October 13–16, in Nice, France.

On being bored and lost (in virtuality)

Kristen Moore and Ehren Helmut Pflugfelder

Department of English, Purdue University, West Lafayette, Indiana, USA

Education in virtual worlds has the potential, it seems, for engaging students in innovative ways and for enabling new discourses on a host of issues. Although virtual spaces are often lauded as 'fun' and 'creative' for students, experiences here are not universal because of the different challenges they present for students. Virtual locations like *Second Life*, *Kaneva*, or *World of Warcraft*, among other multi-user virtual environments (MUVEs), also come with unique challenges for educators as we consider the affordances and risks involved in introducing new technologies into the classroom. Virtual worlds themselves require additional pedagogical and technological scaffolding if they are to function as fun and creative spaces for students. Further, the nuanced interactions of 'real' classroom spaces are sometimes lost in representational virtual spaces. In exploring subject formation and *Second Life*, deWinter and Vie (2008) recognize that 'instructors need to foreground any participation in Second Life with strategies for avoiding or extracting oneself from difficult situations and discussions' (319). We take their suggestion about preparing students for online environments to heart in this viewpoint, and here we focus specifically on the need for pedagogical and technological scaffolding. Our experiences both as students learning in *Second Life* and instructors teaching in virtual environments led us to invent the dialogue below, which reflects the complexities we have encountered. These two characters (Bored and Lost) were inspired from our own experiences as graduate students who were, indeed, bored and lost in virtuality, but in what follows we imagine them as undergraduate students in the composition courses we teach. After each dialogue, we offer a response to how thinking about these students' positions might lead to a more critical pedagogical stance where virtual worlds are concerned.

Bored: Hey, any clue what we're supposed to be doing in here?
Lost: Ummm ... no. Maybe finding the island? I don't even know where I'm at.
Bored: I thought this was going to be cool, but there's just nothing to do.

Lost: And besides, what does this have to do with class?
Bored: I really don't have any clue. I thought I there would be a contest or a game or something.
Lost: Well I haven't seen one, not that I would know what to do if I found it.
Bored: We haven't talked about any of this, have we? Are we just supposed to kill time here?
Lost: Here? This doesn't look like any place I know of.

While many teachers are aware of the benefits of incorporating virtual worlds into their classroom practices, whether as part of specific assignments or as part of larger semester-long goals, we must also consider how we set up our students' entries into virtual worlds. Both students are bored and lost as a consequence of the lack of pedagogical direction – not their own apathy. Bored does not understand the purpose of this assignment, or even if there is a specific assignment, because the virtual space does not prescribe any particular action or directly suggest a narrative for him. Though familiar with game situations, he finds himself without his typical method of engagement. Lost may understand why she is there, though those reasons become less apparent when she tries to use her avatar in the virtual space. Not necessarily familiar with the gaming context, she finds herself suffering from a different issue; while Bored is all-too familiar, though disengaged, she is engaged, though unfamiliar with what is possible in her virtual environment. Both suffer from the lack of explicit or clear scaffolding.

In introducing different activities and tasks in our courses, we have become quite adept at preparing students for complex projects that require adequate preparation on our part. Few experienced instructors, after all, would fail to order assignments without considering their difficulty level. When we employ certain technologies – especially ones we assume will engage students because they are fun and unique – we can fall into the trap of assuming uniqueness will neatly function as pedagogical embeddedness. That is, our assumptions about what is 'cool' or our claims that multimodal, interactive situations can aid learning (see Gee 2007; Shaffer 2006) sometimes blind us to our students' perceptions that what may be 'cool' may also be confusing. In short, novelty does not equal effective educational scaffolding, and we suggest that virtual spaces require a heightened awareness of scaffolding techniques.

When we plan virtual environments in our educational practices, we can constantly ask ourselves: 'will my students know why they are there?' Just as we cannot expect all of our students to come into our subject domains with inherent knowledge, neither can we assume that any virtual space will provide that kind of knowledge. In engaging students in the production of objects, avatars, or discourses, asking them to enact certain narratives, or enabling students to perform research, our pedagogical objectives need to be even more openly expressed than when not working in virtual spaces. Of course, while we do not want to suggest that all activities within virtual environments need to be rigorously monitored and planned, we do suggest that without a strong sense of purpose, many virtual world activities can leave students unaware of how their actions fit into larger learning trajectories.

> Lost: Hey, have you ever been in a virtual world like this? I have no idea how to get around.
> Bored: I play videogames, sometimes, but this isn't nothing like Madden. I know that if you right-click on the 'action' field, you can see one of three options panes. If you review the second pane and then adjust your life levels...
> Lost: I don't feel as if I'm ready for this.
> Bored: What do you mean?
> Lost: I can see what's happening and I can see other people are doing stuff, but I don't know what I can do – what I should be doing.
> Bored: Well ... don't worry, it's not that interesting anyway. There's no real point to it.

While Lost and Bored are clearly thinking through their purpose for being in a virtual space, because of a lack of technological scaffolding, they find themselves searching for connections to familiar software. Bored has played some games before and has a better grasp of how to enter this world; he might navigate this virtual space by relying on what Johnson (2005) refers to as 'probing' and 'telescoping' tactics. Though Lost's ability is less clear, she's certainly more engaged than Bored and could use a more specifically technological tutorial. Despite Bored's advice, which contains a number of steps and terms that might be bewildering to the uninitiated, her motivation, originally higher than Bored's, is waning. The scaffolding that assists our students in understanding why they are there and what they are supposed to be doing must necessarily involve the know-how of engaging with the hardware and software that will be used to accomplish the overall pedagogical aims of the assignment or project. In other words, the technological know-how can not be separate from the pedagogical aims – both must be an intentional part of the teacher's planning and preparation.

Virtual worlds can be idiosyncratic, confusing, and represent a level of technological understanding that may not come easily to those who have not experienced similar interfaces. Learning how to 'right-click' might be an overly simplistic representation of the complex tasks required to interact in virtual worlds, though if we consider the multiple technological strategies required to interact in them, they represent the tip of a large iceberg. Considering functional literacy (Selber 2004), or the basic skills students need prior to gaining rhetorical or critical literacy, causes us to question the practicality of integrating virtual worlds into learning environments without an established technological scaffolding. Students are savvy in their ability to draw upon past experiences in order to adapt to new ones, but because virtual worlds can present a completely different interface, students potentially need technological preparation that complements and anticipates the variety of their current knowledge and experiences.

Importantly, the technological strategies required in virtual worlds might prove quite daunting for students who have limited access to and experience with computers, the internet, and the logic of Web 2.0. While we do not suggest abandoning the possibility of using virtual worlds, we do support a flexible approach to teaching in virtual spaces, where the support offered to students occurs before the moment of expected virtual interaction. DeVoss, Cushman and Grabill (2005) remain advocates of infrastructural analysis, and such an approach might be pertinent to instruction within virtual worlds as well. Education in virtual worlds requires not only the institutional and material infrastructure that DeVoss, Cushman and Grabill emphasize, but also a technological infrastructure that supports the students' individual experiences and needs.

Bored: Have you asked the teacher what we're supposed to do?
Lost: Well, he's up at the front of the room, but he's looking at the screen ... seems to be busy.
Bored: Maybe we can find him in the virtual world.
Lost: Yeah. But that'd require me to know how to get around ... do you have a map?
Bored: There's no map, but he'll see that we don't know what we're doing.
Lost: Will he? Can he tell that I'm just sitting here and that I have no idea what's going on?
Bored: I think so.

In this scenario, Bored and Lost reveal another problem with teaching with virtual locations: that the physical and visual cues we often rely on as teachers and students do not yet persist in virtual spaces. These two students negotiate two separate worlds: one familiar and comfortable and another new and exciting, perhaps, but also unfamiliar and (potentially) daunting. Bored and Lost experience liminality as they learn in a hazy boundary zone, unsure where their normal learning routines fit into virtual worlds. Thus, they wait for their instructor to acknowledge their confusion, but the screen works as a barrier between their 'real' life experiences and the avatars that represent them in virtual world. In such classroom situations, these students do not instigate discussion, but wait passively for their instructor to respond to their unspoken dissatisfaction, confusion, or discomfort.

Bored and Lost remind us that the 'real' experience of students is not easily communicated through virtual spaces and characters. As instructors, how are we to maintain awareness of two worlds at the same time? How can we support our students through the virtual world experience if we, too, are in virtual space? Sarah Robbins, aka intellagirl (http://www.intellagirl.com/), a pioneer of teaching in MUVEs, has shown that *Second Life* and other virtual spaces can be useful for educational purposes (e.g., creating a student-centered environment through virtual activities or engaging students in critical and cultural awareness through avatar development, etc.) (Robbins 2007). We believe, however, that the pedagogy surrounding virtual worlds needs to be fully articulated, especially where teacher–student interactions are concerned.

Avatars lack the nonverbal range and, for us at least, serve as cues for how students are responding to our instruction; they allow us to seize opportune teaching moments and to spontaneously adjust when our approaches are not working effectively. Our experience as students physically in a classroom while learning in a virtual space left us much like Bored and Lost – wondering if our instructor even noticed that we were bored and lost.

As instructors and students, we value alternative approaches to the classroom and multiliteracies. We believe educators need to consider more carefully the pedagogical adaptations necessary when integrating virtual learning into curricula, and here we have tried to delineate some of the major concerns that might require a bit more thought, discussion, and pedagogical awareness. deWinter and Vie (2008) claim that the vague ethical and legal situations of teaching in virtual spaces reflect 'the ways digital technologies are rapidly changing the foundations of our world,' and while this is likely true, our critical response needs to be similarly rapid (319). While we might ask students to engage in virtual spaces in order to illuminate issues in 'our world,' we assert that without a deeper understanding of how to scaffold, engage, and interact with our students in these new worlds, we run the risk of doing them a particular disservice, potentially leaving them bored and/or lost.

References

DeVoss, D.N., E. Cushman, and J.T. Grabill. 2005. Infrastructure and composing: The when of new-media writing. *College Composition and Communication* 57: 14–44.

deWinter, A., and S. Vie. 2008. Press enter to 'say': Using *Second Life* to teach critical literacy. *Computers and Composition* 25: 313–22.

Gee, J.P. 2007. *What video games have to teach us about learning and literacy.* New York: Palgrave.

Johnson, S. 2005. *Everything bad is good for you.* New York: Penguin.

Robbins, S. 2007. *Using a multi-user virtual environment (MUVE) for education: One instructor's adventure in* Second Life. Elearning Guild 360 report on games and education. http://www.elearningguild.com/research/archives/index.cfm?action=viewonly2&id=121

Selber, S. 2004. *Multiliteracies for a digital age.* Carbondale: Southern Illinois University Press.

Shaffer, D.W. 2006. *How computer games help children learn.* New York: Palgrave.

Index

Page numbers in *Italics* represent tables.
Page numbers in **Bold** represent figures.

AC3D 117
ActiveWorlds 53–4, 77
Age of Conan(R) 84, 91
Aion(R) 94, 96
Aldrich, C. 14
All is Full of Love (Bjork): Cunningham music video 15
Anderson, T.: Archer, W. and Garrison, D. 79
Andros Barrier Reef 148
Ang, C.: Zaphiris, P. and Pfeil, U. 108
Anglia Ruskin University, Cambridge 14
Apple University Consortium 115; *Mac OSX* 115
Apple UNIX 118
Archer, W.: Garrison, D. and Anderson, T. 79
Ars Virtua Gallery 9
Association of Internet Researchers (AoIR) 5
asynchronous learning 34–5
Athens University 84
AutoCAD 141
avatars 10–17, **12**, 24–6, 36, 55, 71–2, 120–4, 135–7, 156; representations of 96, 109, *see also* Kriti Island; *Second Life*

Banff Centre, Canada 9; Art and Virtual Environments project 9
Barab, S.: *et al* 150
Bignell, S. 14
Blackboard 52–4
blogs 48, 53–4, 58–9
Bogost, I. 133
bored and lost (in virtuality): and pedagogical direction 152–6
Boston City Council (UK) 109
British Broadcasting Corporation (BBC) 47; One Big Weekend concert 49
Brown, B.: Laurier, E. and Reeves, S. 86

Calende race 91
CAVE automatic virtual environment 2
chat logger script 124
The Chronicle of Higher Education 142
Clark, S.: and Maher, L. 20

collaborative virtual environments (CVEs) 148–9
Collins, C.: and Jenning, N. 8
Community of Inquiry Model 79, 82
Computer Animation Degree Show 56–7
constructivist learning 110–11, 124–6
Cornell Land Use Game (CLUG) 134
Counter Strike(R) 86
Creative Commons 66–7
Cross, J. 34
Cunningham, C. 15
Current TV 62
Cushman, E.: Grabill, J. and DeVoss, D. 155
cybernetics 133–4

De Freitas, S. 15–16
Dead in Iraq (DeLappe) 10
DeLappe, J. 10
Dell 47, 49
Design Games (Sanoff) 134
Design of Learning Spaces in 3D Virtual Environments (DELVE) 20–42
DeVoss, D.: Cushman, E. and Grabill, J. 155
deWinter, A.: and Vie, S. 152, 156
Dickey, M. 87
Digital Games Research Association (Digra) 5
Dillenbourg, P. 82
DotA(R) 84, 91
Doyle, D. 7–18
Ducheneaut, N.: *et al* 89, 93–5, 99; and Moore, R. 90–2

Emerson College, Boston 109
European Institute of Business (INSEAD) 8
EVE Online(R) 84, 89–101

Facebook 48, 53, 84
Feldt, A. 134
Filene, P. 136
Flickr 53, 109
Frensch, P.: and Sternberg, R. 80

INDEX

Gaia Online 43
Galarneau, L. 80
Galloway, A. 135
gaming courses 134–5
Garrison, D. 82; Anderson, T. and Archer, W. 79
Gee, J. 78, 90, 132–3
Google Earth 114–17, 122–4; library model **117**
Google SketchUp 114–19, 124; Lower Mill Site library **116**
Gordon, E.: and Koo, G. 109
Gough, N.: Jin, L. and Wen, Z. 46–60
Grabill, J.: DeVoss, D. and Cushman, E. 155
Grasshopper (Linklater) 15
Green, A.: and McKenna, K. 2
Greenberg, S. 81–2
Griffiths, J. 8
Griffiths, M.: Meredith, A. and Hussain, Z. 86
grinding 79

Habbo Hotel 43
Harris, J.: and Nardi, B. 94, 97–8
Hedlund, G.: and Nonaka, I. 62–3
Hendricks, F. 134
Herbert Gallery, Coventry 13; *Fact or Fiction* exhibition 13; *Something that I'll Never Really See* (V&A) exhibition 13
Heumann, L.: and Wetmore, L. 131
HiPiHi 43
Hollander, J.: and Thomas, D. 130–45
Hub2 109
Huffaker, D.: et al 85
Hunsinger, J.: and Krotoski, A. 1–6
Hussain, Z.: Griffiths, M. and Meredith, A. 86

IBM 47
Ichijo, K.: Von Krogh, G. and Nonaka, I. 62–4, 70
identity and intellectual property 59
Immersed in Learning (University of Wolverhampton) 7–18
instant messaging (IM) 37, 48, 50
International Symposium for Electronic Arts (ISEA) 7, 13
Internet Research 8.0: Let's Play (Vancouver) 1

Jenning, N.: and Collins, C. 8
Jin, L.: Wen, Z. and Gough, N. 46–60
John D. and Catherine T. MacArthur Foundation 132
Johnson, S. 154
Joint Information Systems Committee (JISC) 20
Jonassen, D.: Peck, K. and Wilson, B. 110, 125
Jones, D. 9, 16
Joy of Teaching (Filene) 136

Kaneva 152
knowledge exchange 61–75; activists mobilisation 65, 68–9; case study 63–72; creation and vision 63–70; data-flow model **64**; globalizing 66, 70; managing conversations 65, 68, 72; right context 65–6, 69–70; and *Second Life* 61–75
Komis, V.: and Voulgari, I. 76–106
Koo, G.: and Gordon, E. 109
Koster, R. 93
Kriti Island 7–18; creation 8–9; *Fact or Fiction* student exhibition 11–13, **12–13**; seminar space 13–15
Krotoski, A.: and Hunsinger, J. 1–6

Laurier, E.: Reeves, S. and Brown, B. 86
Lazzaro, N. 89
learning: asynchronous 34–5
Learning Management System (LMS) 52–4; *Blackboard* 52–4
Learning and Research in Second Life (Hunsinger and Krotoski) 1
learning spaces design investigation 19–45; activity-focused 26–7; educator authority 35–6; further research 42–3; implications and design principles 39–43, *40–1*; indoor and outdoor spaces and sandboxes 23–6, **23–4, 26**; interpretation 23–8, 40; interruption avoidance 38–9; key research questions (RQs) 21–3, 28–33; pedagogy relationship 28–9, 40–2; real-world-like settings 25; seating arrangements 36–8, **36**; and *Second Life* 19–44; socialisation and community building 35; study aim, data and methodology 21–2; visual realism and flexibility 29–33, **30–2**, 40; within an island 34–8, 41
learnscapes 34
Leeson, Lynn Hershman 9
Left4Dead(R) 84
Lessig, R.S. 66–7
Lester, J. 1
Liberate your Avatar (Sermon) 9–10
Linden Labs 1, 7; Education liaison 1, *see also* Second Life
Lineage II(R) 76, 83–4, 87–99; peer mentoring and academies 94–6
Linklater, R. 15

Mac OSX 115
McCulloch, M.: Mitchell, W. and Purcell, P. 135

INDEX

machinima 9; course/project 65–70
McKenna, K.: and Green, A. 2
McLuhan, M. 71
Madison (2200) 133
Magerko, B. 146
Maher, L.: and Clark, S. 20
Mallan, K.: *et al* 107–29
manipulation space 125
Manovich, L. 14
Marlboro College, Vermont 35
Massively Multi-User Workshop (MML08) 14
massively multiplayer online role-playing games (MMORPS) 2, 49, 76–106; characters, roles and competition 92–3, 95–6; collaborative interactions environment features *83*; communication 96–7, 100–3; conceptual framework 78–80; defining the expert 85–6; groups and decision-making 97–101; learning and motivation 86–9; limitations 101–3; narrative 91; problem solving 77–8, 80–2, 101–3; research methodology 82–4; sociability, cooperation and collaboration 93–6, 100–3; task-oriented interactions and design 82, 89–90
Mayer, R. 80–1, 148
Meadows, M. 16–17
Mediamatics 62
MediaZone island (*Second Life*) 66
Meredith, A.: Hussain, Z. and Griffiths, M. 86
metaverse 7–9
Microsoft Windows 118
Minocha, S.: and Reeves, A. 19–45
Mitchell, W.: Purcell, P. and McCulloch, M. 135
The Model Cities program 133–4
Moore, K.: and Pflugfelder, E. 152–6
Moore, R.: and Ducheneaut, N. 90–2
Mori, Masahiro: Uncanny Valley 15–16, **16**, 148
multi-player online games (MMO) 108
multi-user virtual environments (MUVE) 108, 152–6
MySpace 48, 53

Nardi, B.: and Harris, J. 94, 97–8
Nash, A. 10–11
National Aeronautics and Space Administration (NASA) 50; *Second Life* Colab 50
National Oceanographic and Atmospheric Administration (NOAA) 50
non-player characters (NPCs) 86
Nonaka, I.: and Hedlund, G. 62–3; Ichijo, K. and Von Krogh, G. 62–4, 70
Norton, P.: and Wiburg, K. 81

Ogre Exporter 118
Ondrejka, C. 52
Open Sim 43, 118
Open University: *Open Life* (*Second Life*) 24, 38–9; *OUtopia* (*Second Life*) 38–9
OpenSimulator 114
Operative Virtual Campus (*Second Life*) 8

Pankhurst, Emily 10
Patras University 84
Peck, K.: Wilson, B. and Jonassen, D. 110, 125
Pfeil, U.: Ang, C. and Zaphiris, P. 108
Pflugfelder, E.: and Moore, K. 152–6
Planning Operational Gaming Experiment (POGE) 134
player versus environment (PvE) 79, 99, 102
player versus player (PvP) 79, 96, 99; tasks 89–90
Polar Express (Zemeckis) 15
Purcell, P.: McCulloch, M. and Mitchell, W. 135

Rauterberg, M. 94
real-life buildings: replicas 20
RealXtend (RX) 117–18
Reeves, A.: and Minocha, S. 19–45
Reeves, S.: Brown, B. and Laurier, E. 86
Reflective Virtual Campus (*Second Life*) 8
Regenerative Presence (Leeson) 9
Representing Reality (seminar) 14
Ricoeur, P. 121
Rive, P.: and Thomassen, A. 61–75
Robbins, S. 155
A Rose Heard at Dusk (Nash) 10–11
Ryan, M. 121–3

Salt March to Dandi (DeLappe) 10
Sanoff, H.: *Design Games* 134
SchomeBase (*Second Life*) 24
Schon, D. 131
Second Life 1–5, 77, 152–6; as augmented learning platform 46–59; creativity and practice 9–11; Info Island 5; knowledge exchange and design education 61–75; learning spaces design 19–44; Lower Mill Site replica **119**; *MediaZone* island 66; NASA Colab 50; Open University islands 24, 38–9; Operative Virtual Campus 8; Reflective Virtual Campus 8; *SchomeBase* 24; SciLands 5; *Studio Wikitecture* 109; Toyota 49; *TSL* project 117; vandalism 137; Visit Mexico **30**, *see also* Kriti Island; urban planning
Serious Games Initiative (Woodrow Wilson International Center for Scholars) 132–4, 139

INDEX

Sermon, P. 9–10
Shaffer, D. 133, 142
SimCity 134, 139
SketchUp™ 141
Slogbase 124
Sloodle 37
Snow Crash (Stephenson) 7–8
social virtual worlds (SVWs) 46–60; augmented learning platform 46–59, *58*; comparison *54*; e-tutoring/e-mentoring 55–6; innovative characteristics 50–1; as learning environments 50–1; networking 48–51; prototyped learning practices 53–7; role-playing simulation 57; student-centred active learning 56–7
socio-constructivism 27–8, 41–2
Spensley, D.C. 10
Star Wars Galaxies 90
Starry Night (Van Gogh/Wright) 9
Stephenson, N. 7–8
Sternberg, R.: and Frensch, P. 80
Structure from Motion (SFM) 3D geometric model 147–8
Studio Wikitecture: Second Life 109
studio-based learning 130–45; key benefits and questions 131–2, *140*, 142–3; role of computer games 132–4; teaching planning case study 134–42; unique qualities 131–2
Survey Monkey 21

technology enhanced learning (TEL) 46–60; augmented platform design 51–3, **52**; and social virtual worlds 46–59
text as game 110–11, 123
There 53–4
Thomas, D.: and Hollander, J. 130–45
Thomassen, A.: and Rive, P. 61–75
Toyota 47; Scion xB and Second Life 49
Tribal Wars(R) 83–4, 89–92, 97; forum excerpt 98

Uncanny Valley (Mori) 15–16, **16**, 148
UNIX (Apple) 118
urban planning 107–29; analysis and topics of interest *113*; collaborative learning 124–7, **126**; Lower Mill Site context and setting 111–27, **112**, **116**, **117**; methodology 112–13; play 122–4; technical 115–19; textual and design 119–22; theoretical framework 110–11; time-space-place 120–2; virtual studio 130–45, **137–8**; workshop questions and approach 109–10, 114, *see also* Second Life

vandalism: *Second Life* 137
very large scale integration (VLSI) 146
Victoria University, Wellington 62

Vie, S.: and deWinter, A. 152, 156
virtual environments (VEs) 146–51; ecosystems 147–9; future work and issues 149–50
virtual learning environments (VLEs) 20, 47–59
virtual worlds (VWs) 1–6; background 108–10; creative practice 7–18; design of learning spaces 19–45; global opportunities 4–5; histories 2–3; learning centred environments 4; research 3, *see also* social virtual worlds (SVWs)
Virtually U (Jenning and Collins) 8
Voice over Internet Protocol (VoIP) 97
Von Krogh, G.: Nonaka, I. and Ichijo, K. 62–4, 70
Voulgari, I.: and Komis, V. 76–106

War Poets Online (DeLappe) 10
Warburton, S. 108
Web (2.0) 155
Wen, Z.: Gough, N. and Jin, L. 46–60
Westminster University 55–6, 135; London Gallery West degree show 56–7, **57**; virtual campus **55**
The West(R) 84
Wetmore, L.: and Heumann, L. 131
Wiburg, K.: and Norton, P. 81
Wikipedia 51
wikis 48, 51–4, 58
Wilson, B.: Jonassen, D. and Peck, K. 110, 125
Wilson, F. 134
Wolverhampton University: Digital Media Programme modules 13–15; *Immersed in Learning* 7–18
Woodrow Wilson International Center for Scholars 132; Serious Games Initiative 132–4, 139
World of Warcraft(R) 20, 84, 87–101, 132, 152
Wright, R. 9

Yee, N. 95
Young, M. 81
YouTube 48, 53–4, 58, 109

Zaphiris, P.: Pfeil, U. and Ang, C. 108
ZeroG Skydancers III 10

www.routledge.com/9780415693417

Related titles from Routledge

Everyday Ethics
Reflections on Practice

Edited by Gretchen B. Rossman and Sharon F. Rallis

Everyday Ethics looks at the moments that demand moral consideration and ethical choice that arise as part of a researcher's daily practice. Drawing on principles of systematic inquiry as transparent and grounded in conceptual reasoning, it describes research as praxis and the researcher as practitioner. The researcher is a decision-maker for both procedural and ethical matters that attend the conduct of research, especially when the research is focused on human wellbeing. Every decision about data collection, analysis, interpretation, and presentation has moral dimensions. This book invites us to deepen our understanding of everyday ethics, and contributes to the ongoing discourse about research as moral practice, conducted by such reflexive practitioners.

This book was originally published as a special issue of the *International Journal of Qualitative Studies in Education*.

December 2011: 246 x 174: 136pp
Hb: 978-0-415-69341-7
£80 / $125

For more information and to order a copy visit
www.routledge.com/9780415693417

Available from all good bookshops

www.routledge.com/9780415693233

Related titles from Routledge

Inquiry into the Future of Lifelong Learning in the UK
An Internationa Analysis

Edited by Peter Jarvis

This volume offers a comprehensive international response to the National Institute of Adult Continuing Education (NIACE)'s inquiry into the future of lifelong learning in the UK. The book focuses upon some of the main themes of the inquiry, and analyses them from very broad perspectives undertaken by some of the world's leading scholars. It provides an excellent introduction to significant debates about lifelong learning such as ecology, migration, morality, happiness and poverty. Each chapter raises issues of policy and practice, with clear areas of discussion, thus assisting readers in truly engaging with the issues. The final chapter contains a response by Tom Schuller, one of the NIACE's inquiry authors. This book is essential reading for students of lifelong learning, especially educational policy makers.

This book was originally published as a special issue of the *International Journal of Lifelong Education*.

November 2011: 246 x 174: 128pp
Hb: 978-0-415-69323-3
£80 / $125

For more information and to order a copy visit
www.routledge.com/9780415693233

Available from all good bookshops

www.routledge.com/9780415693240

Related titles from Routledge

Internationalization of Teacher Education

Creating Globally Competent Teachers and Teacher Educators for the 21st Century

Edited by Reyes L. Quezada

This book proposes to excite readers to engage in conversations on how Schools and Colleges of Education can internationalize teacher education programs so that graduates have global teaching experiences, that teacher education curricula include global perspectives, and that there are opportunities to have faculty think and teach from a global perspective. The contributors in this book have the knowledge and expertise in international teacher education to answer many questions regarding the development of a 21st century competent global teaching force. They describe their experiences, programs, and support for the goal of continuing to internationalize Schools and Colleges of Education. The book is designed to be interactive - readers are encouraged to engage themselves in the conversation as the editor invites them to e-mail any of the authors to discuss questions posed.

This book was originally published as a special issue of *Teaching Education*.

November 2011: 246 x 174: 128pp
Hb: 978-0-415-69324-0
£80 / $125

For more information and to order a copy visit
www.routledge.com/9780415693240

Available from all good bookshops

www.routledge.com/9780415676625

Related titles from Routledge

Principles for Effective Pedagogy
International Responses to Evidence from the UK Teaching & Learning Research Programme

Edited by Mary James and Andrew Pollard

The UK Teaching and Learning Research Programme (TLRP) worked for ten years to improve outcomes for learners in schools and other sectors through high quality research. One outcome of individual projects and across-Programme thematic work was the development of ten 'evidence-informed' principles for effective pedagogy. Synopses of these principles have been widely disseminated, particularly to practitioners. However, the evidence and reasoning underpinning them has not yet been fully explained. This book fills this gap by providing a scholarly account of the research evidence that informed the development of these principles, as well as offering some evidence of early take-up and impact. It also includes responses from highly-respected researchers throughout the world in order to locate the work in the broader international literature, to extend it by drawing on similar work elsewhere, to provide critique and to stimulate further development and debate.

This book was originally published as a special issue of *Research Papers in Education*.

December 2011: 246 x 174: 136pp
Hb: 978-0-415-67662-5
£80 / $125

For more information and to order a copy visit
www.routledge.com/9780415676625

Available from all good bookshops

www.routledge.com/9780415697477

Related titles from Routledge

Understanding Creative Uses of ICTs
Users as Social Actors

Edited by David Kurt Herold, Harmeet Sawhney and Leopoldina Fortunati

The disjuncture between the design intent of the developers of ICTs and the needs of the users has often led to surprising use of new technologies, as users have refused to become mere agents of the designers. Individual users have adopted their own uses of ICTs based on the complex webs of relations and meanings in which they function as social actors. Instead of adjusting these webs to new ICTs, they have fit the ICTs into their pre-existing social webs, often resulting in imaginative and creative uses of new technologies, not envisaged by the original designers.

The contributions in this volume provide studies of such integrations of ICTs into the lives of human users, and demonstrate that such uses should not be regarded as 'faulty' or 'mistaken', merely because they 'fail' to meet the expectations of the original designers of the ICTs. Instead, human users should be given precedence over ICTs, and the creative uses of 'universal' technologies by individual users should be emphasised and studied.

This book was originally published as special issue of *The Information Society*.

February 2012: 276 x 219: 120pp
Hb: 978-0-415-69747-7
£80 / $125

For more information and to order a copy visit
www.routledge.com/9780415697477

Available from all good bookshops